BELIEVE IN YOUR BUSINESS

HOW TO GENERATE GROWTH BY SQUEEZING A LEMON

Gaynor Lawton

Belief strategist and lemon squeezer

First published by Busybird Publishing 2019

Copyright © 2019 Gaynor Lawton

ISBN 978-1-925940-04-0

All rights reserved. No part of this publication may be reproduced, distributed or transmitted in any form or by any means without the written permission of the author. This publication is purely opinion, suggestion and recommendation. The author takes no responsibility for any changes that may occur in the reader's situation. The decision to carry out the exercises and processes is solely that of the reader and does not guarantee that their situation will change or that their business will grow. All exercises and processes are deemed safe when carried out as outlined in this book.

The material in this publication is of the nature of general comment and does not represent professional advice. Readers should obtain professional advice where appropriate, before making any decisions. To the maximum extent permitted by law, the author disclaims all responsibility and liability to any person, arising directly or indirectly from any person taking or not taking action based on the information in this publication.

www.believeinyourbusiness.info

Cover design: Gaynor Lawton
Layout and typesetting: Busybird Publishing
Editor: Anna Bilbrough

Busybird Publishing
2/118 Para Road
Montmorency, Victoria
Australia 3094
www.busybird.com.au

This book is dedicated to Roubini, Lady Layla and Jackson Brown, who together make up our quirky little family. Thank you for choosing me.

Also to my friend and colleague Tasha Rees, who has shown great courage through her journey with Crohn's disease and then cancer. You are the strongest person I know.

Thank you

There are many people who have contributed to the manifesting of *Believe in Your Business*:

My bestie Kara DeJong, who spent hours listening to my ideas over the years.

My Greek family, whose arms are forever welcoming and whose table is always overflowing. Your support is more than I could wish for.

Three of my official 'test pilots', Nicki K, Dar B and James H, who *tried and tested* all the exercises as outlined in this book during an intensive twelve weeks.

Numerous other friends and acquaintances who were subjected to my random conversations and a-ha moments and who inadvertently tested processes for me in the most unexpected places – you know who you are and I thank you for your ears, shoulders, feedback and support.

The generous Kickstarter campaign donors

Below is the list of generous contributors to our very successful crowdfunding campaign, who raised funds to help part-fund the publishing of this book. You certainly gave me the final nudge of motivation to jump. All contributors are listed below in alphabetical order by first name.

Thank you to:

Amanda Wood
Anna Clements
Blaise Van Hecke
Brian McTaggart
Cameron Rambert
Cherri Ashana
Cindy Rochstein
Dar Bryers
Dina Karvess
George Karavassilis
Granger Estate Agents
Greg Vercoe
Jann Hill
Jeannet Faber
Jim Karvess
John Miyasato
Kara DeJong
Katherine Karvess
Liesl Bartjes-Harvey
Madeleine McGrath
Nick Cook
Nicki Kuurman
Orna Silas
Renee Kalissa
Rondelle Douglas
Rowena Rose
Ryan Pedley
Sonja Leon
Sue A
Vanessa Ecroyd
Vincent Lazzara

Contents

Foreword	1
Preface	7
1 - Introduction	11
2 - Measures	25
3 - Identifying Your Beliefs	39
G = Ground Work	
4 - Laying Your Own Foundations	63
R = Rejection	
5 - Bouncing Back	75
O = Outcome	
6 - The Road Ahead	95
W = Worth	
7 - For What it's Worth	123
T = Trust	
8 - Is it Luck?	139
H = Habits	
9 - The Winds of Change	153
10 - Letting Go of Beliefs	167
11 - Revisiting Your Measures	185
12 - Moving Forward	189
Afterword	193
Freelance Australia Pty Ltd	197
References	201
The professional services used	205
About the Author	207

Know your lemon juice

'If you cannot do great things, do small things in a great way.'

Napoleon Hill, author, 1888 – 1970.

Foreword

As an entrepreneur, can you imagine coming to the end of your life and looking back to find no discernible regrets? No missed opportunities ... could you *believe* that to be possible?

That very question is asking you to suspend any scepticism you may have about your business and lets you live, if only for a moment, in the realms of possibility and *what if?*

Gaynor Lawton is asking you to do the same. By laying out the foundations of how our brain works, and implementing her G.R.O.W.T.H model, she is laying down the ground work for you to play within that magical place, and by doing so, giving you the opportunity to achieve your career goals. Who wouldn't want that?

According to Socrates, organised knowledge is the oldest profession in the world. People who can take complicated information and organise it in a way that is easy to absorb is essentially what every business is, at its core.

However, finding someone who can deliver relevant and easy-to-implement information is a lot harder to do.

I met Gaynor in a seminar about spirituality. It was a small group led by a mutual acquaintance of ours. The content was engaging but it was Gaynor's input that added a layer of depth and understanding for everyone present. As I got to know her better following the seminar, I realised that she approached life and business in the same manner: she lays down easy foundations for people to build upon.

Gaynor can take whatever transformation goal you desire for your business, and design the systems, tools and strategies that can turn it into something applicable, digestible, and achievable. Nowhere is this more apparent than within the pages of the book that you are holding.

Not only does she make it achievable, she is able to, once again, take vast amounts of difficult and complicated information, and turn it into something engaging and relevant to everyone from the entrepreneur to the start-up business owner, to anyone looking to ascend to the next level of achievement within their life. Gaynor is able to suspend her own scepticism and hold the space so you can move forward with grace and certainty.

Personal anecdotes, reflections and realisations from Gaynor's private life enrich the contents and we are better

Foreword

able to discern similar learnings from our own experiences. It is the generosity of the author that allows us to find our own path and understandings on how our beliefs dominate, and shape, our own lives.

If organised knowledge is the oldest profession, then belief must be the oldest business strategy, because – let's face it – nothing is created without it.

Get ready to transform your business and, as a happy by-product, your world. This book will change how you see yourself, your business, and let you play a bigger game than you could ever *believe* ...

Fiona Stuart
Founder & CEO
DivorceCoach.com

'No-one ever made a difference by being like everybody else.'

P.T Barnum, showman and founder of Barnum & Bailey Circus, 1810 – 1891.

Preface

We're All Lemons!

Every morning I squeeze half a lemon into a cup of hot water and sip it to cleanse my body. I can guarantee the only thing that will come out of that lemon is *lemon juice* (and the occasional pip). How do I know this? Because the only thing inside a lemon is its juice – not orange juice, coffee or a bar of chocolate, thankfully.

Imagine you are a lemon. If you were squeezed (challenged) what would come out of you? *That's* what you're about to find out. If you like what comes out – your response, action, behaviour – fantastic. If you don't like what comes out, now's your opportunity to change it. The most relevant part of this process is to understand that the way you respond when challenged *must* have been inside you because that's what came out, and that response, like all behaviours and actions, stems from a belief you carry.

Knowing your lemon juice can help you become conscious of everything you do. Nobody can *make* you feel, do or act in any particular way: *you* decide how *you* behave. Often we are unaware of what's inside us – until we are squeezed or challenged. This book is going to gently challenge you. It is your job to observe your lemon juice – what you feel, think and how you act when faced with each challenge. Through observing this behaviour you can then recognise the underlying belief and decide whether to manage, change or remove that belief, which invariably will be restricting you in some way.

Once you become aware of what you believe about yourself, your business and the world you live in, you will begin to see what you can do to change things. Often just a tweak can create a huge ripple effect. Understanding the influence you and your beliefs have on the development of your business is enough, but changing or even removing those beliefs is more beneficial and can create a great impact in your business and on you as a business owner.

Enjoy being squeezed!

'Your time is limited so don't waste it living someone else's life.'

Steve Jobs, co-founder of Apple, 1955 – 2011.

Chapter 1

Introduction

Are you a business owner, business leader, influencer or innovator who has taken the leap into entrepreneurship only to discover your strong work ethic and network of contacts isn't enough to build a successful business? Then you are reading the right book.

Believe in Your Business is based around two concepts: beliefs and relationships. A belief is a thought that you think so many times it becomes real or true to you. A relationship is the interaction between you and *something* else – not just *someone* else. That relationship, whether it's with a person, the traffic, work, food or your computer, is shaped by the beliefs you have about it and yourself.

I grew up in a working class family in the North West region of England. My father was a factory worker at Vauxhall Motors for most of his life. He left just short of his retirement to pursue painting and decorating homes, which he loved. My mum always worked too, sometimes at a job, sometimes for herself. At one time, she owned a wool shop selling knitting yarns and haberdashery items. I was still at primary school, but I remember helping her display the window and deciding I wanted to be a window dresser. Watching my parents working and sometimes struggling to make ends meet instilled a solid work ethic in me. My brother and two sisters have also adopted this work ethic. What it also did was expose me to a set of beliefs around having to work hard to make money and therefore limited the way I believed money could be obtained. So, armed with a positive attitude and enthusiastic persona, I set off into the world of employment. First stop: Barclays Bank, a far cry from window dressing. The irony of my first job being at a bank is not lost on me.

It took me moving permanently to Australia at the age of 38 to actually start my own business.

One of the greatest challenges I faced, and I have since realised most business owners face to some extent, was my lack of belief in my own ability.

When my business started, it was built around offering marketing consulting and business development to start-up and small business owners. It naturally developed into business mentoring and I began to facilitate workshops and monthly networking events.

Introduction

Lack of self-belief was becoming more prominent in the clients I was attracting, which caused me to take a look at myself. I clearly saw in my clients what I initially couldn't see in myself: under-utilised talent, potential and passion.

I watched as some clients gave up their dream of running a business and reluctantly returned to employment. I knew that, whatever I discovered, that was not an option for me. I have always had a deep knowing that my purpose is to inspire and motivate people, and I feel I have done this successfully, if not consistently, throughout my life. This prevalence of self-doubt caused me to research further and I discovered self-doubt is in fact an epidemic that is paralyzing society on a global scale.

In 2017, *The Dove Global Girls Beauty and Confidence Report* interviewed 10,500 females across 13 countries and found that women's confidence in their bodies is on a steady decline. The report highlighted that, regardless of dividing factors like age or geography, low body esteem has become a unifying challenge shared by women and girls around the world.

The 2017 report builds on two previous studies by Dove from 2004 and 2010. As stated in the report findings, eight in ten women said they would opt out of important life activities (being with family and friends or trying out for sports teams) when they didn't feel good about the way they look (*The Dove Global Girls Beauty and Confidence Report*, 2017). With more than a third of businesses in Australia and America owned by women, these statistics are clearly going to impact their performance in the workplace (Tattersall 2018; *The 2017 State of Women-Owned Businesses Report* 2017).

Men are quietly suffering too. The BetterHealth Channel states, 'around 11% of Australian men are on a weight loss diet at any given time, and it is thought that around one third of people with an eating disorder are male (although it is likely that this is under-reported)'.

At the Centre for Appearance Research (CAR) at the University of West England (UWA) research revealed that men have high levels of anxiety about their bodies and that some resort to compulsive exercise, strict diets, laxatives or making themselves sick in an attempt to lose weight or achieve a more toned physique. Almost 81% talked about their own or others' appearance in ways that drew attention to weight, lack of hair or a slim frame. 30% have heard someone refer to their 'beer belly', 19% have been described as 'chubby' and 19% have overheard talk about their 'man boobs'. And 23% said concerns about their appearance had deterred them from going to the gym. Again, this has to be affecting their performance at work.

Introduction

According to their article *With Superheroes Comes the Pressure of Unrealistic Male Bodies*, healthline.com reports that there's one major contributing factor that can be credited for the rise of negative body perception for men and boys: the silver screen.

In the article Raj Chander wrote, 'The media tells men that we should be lean, strong, and muscular. But the male body image struggle is about more than the shape of our bodies. Among other concerns, men are figuring out how to deal with hair loss, height perception, and skin care.

'The hair loss industry alone is estimated to be worth $1.5 billion. No thanks to the stigma, men with thinning or no hair may face the stereotype that they're less attractive, agreeable, and assertive. Research has also found that hair loss is linked to feelings of inadequacy, depression, stress, and low self-esteem.

As for height, data indicates that people associate taller men with higher levels of charisma, education or leadership qualities, increased career success, and even a more robust dating life.'

These findings excited me because I knew that developing self-belief had the potential to change lives. I began by exploring my own beliefs and immediately saw how I was continually repeating the same patterns, how I was attracting certain types of clients, I never seemed to be able to make more than a certain amount of money each month, I helped everyone whether they wanted helping or not. My greatest realisation was my need to prove to the world I could do it all alone. What I saw was my patterns were affecting *all* areas of my life. It's impossible to have a belief that only affects certain parts of your life; in some ways, that belief impacts a whole life.

The essence of this book is to help you, male or female, become aware of the power of who you really are and how, by recognising your hidden beliefs, you will see why your business is as it is and how easily you can change it. My aim is to show you how to *consciously choose the next chapter of your life*.

My search for ways to change my beliefs began.

I read anything and everything I could find about the belief system. There was a common message running through most of it – that the way to change a belief was to override it with a new, more positive one. This worked – providing I didn't forget to reinstate the new belief on a very regular basis. Of course, when things were running smoothly it felt like the new belief was working so the motivation to continue repeating it lessened.

Introduction

Once the continuous overriding slowed down it wasn't long before my old, original belief reappeared.

This concept wasn't working for me. I would be halfway through my day and realise I hadn't practised my new belief affirmation. I knew beliefs were blocks of energy and, having had some amazing experiences with healing energy, I set out to create a way of removing the energy of a belief so that it was no longer in the energy field.

After many attempts I finally settled on a way that is simple and does not require any tools. It can be done discreetly in a room full of people or alone. The impact is immediate. I continued to work on removing my own beliefs until I saw significant change in my patterns of behaviour. When I knew something had changed in me, I began to use the concept on my friends and then my clients and watched as they made progress in areas they had previously struggled.

To be able to recognise your patterns you have to become aware of your thoughts. To help you do this I've developed a series of exercises and processes presented in this book to appeal to all types of business owners – the closed-minded, the spiritually aware, the left-brainers and the right-brainers. These processes can be as practical and non-spiritual or as energy-focused and spiritual as you want them to be – either way you will see a difference – giving you the *choice* to make a change, or not.

I rebranded my entire business and refocused my *why* to shine a light on helping people discover the old and often hidden beliefs they harbor. Beliefs influence our decision-making and give us a distorted perception of who we are. This has led to the *believe* message being delivered in workshops, mentoring, podcasts, annual retreats, and this, the first in the series of *Believe* books.

Believe in Your Business contains a range of exercises and processes delivered in six chapters built around the acronym G.R.O.W.T.H.

Chapter 4 **G is for Ground Work** – When you run a business or lead a team in business it is vital you know where your own strengths lie.

Chapter 5 **R is for Rejection** – Learn to handle this and your business landscape will change.

Chapter 6 **O is for Outcome** – Where are you heading? It helps to know what you're aiming for.

Chapter 7 **W is for Wealth** – Getting comfortable with money will strengthen your purpose.

Chapter 8 **T is for Trust** – You have chosen this path for a reason, trust in the journey.

Introduction

Chapter 9 **H is for Habits** – Create new habits that lead to positive behaviours.

The topics chosen for each exercise within the G.R.O.W.T.H chapters don't always refer to work or business. This is intentional to prevent you from pre-empting answers and becoming too comfortable. If an exercise reveals you as a procrastinator it is fair to say you will be a procrastinator in your business and personal life.

I first heard the statement, 'The way you do something, is the way you do everything,' during one of my early yoga classes. I began doing gentle rehabilitation yoga after my face paralyzed in 2012 due to the accumulation of stress. I was new to yoga and I wasn't quite sure what my teacher was referring to. She explained that I was definitely *committed* and *determined* and was putting in lots of *effort* – great qualities for business, not so necessary for yoga. Over time, I became familiar with my patterns of behaviour – every one of which I could justify. What yoga did was change the way I approached a challenge – not just the yoga challenges, life challenges too – and this added greatly to my research.

I see my role as a belief strategist as a way of enabling you to discover what you *believe* to be true about you, your life and the world you live in. Once you are aware of your beliefs and can see how some can restrict your growth, you can *choose* what to do next.

How will this help grow your business?

When you uncover what you really believe about money, your competitors and your customers, you will see why your business is as it is.

The great news is this book gives you two very significant strategies that when implemented can change the course of your business and even your life. The first strategy shows you how to *recognise* your beliefs – they are often so embedded in the subconscious mind that you are completely unaware of them. The second strategy shows you how to remove any unwanted beliefs.

As you work through this book one chapter at a time, completing the exercises and implementing them into your daily life, you will change what you *usually* do. What you do instead becomes a conscious choice. All the suggested exercises require a degree of practise, some more than others. Set your intention that you want to make a change in your usual routine and it will help keep you focused and cement that change sooner.

I have lived every exercise and process suggested in these pages – I had to in order to deliver them with complete knowing and confidence that they work.

Introduction

In doing so, I have a greater sense of my own value; I have an increased amount of abundance in my life, in every area. I have become aware of and changed my natural instinct to fix everybody else's problems. I learnt the hard way that it is a thankless exercise – most people with problems don't actually want them fixed and those that do will ask for help. I also recently learnt that asking for help and accepting help can make friendships deeper, bring family closer, or reveal and end inauthentic relationships – all of which I am humbled by and deeply grateful for.

I found the confidence to seek out the right business coach for me. It took me over 12 months to ask her because I *believed* I wasn't good enough to be her client. Not only did she say yes, she also agreed to write the foreword of this book. I have also learnt to appreciate that setbacks and rejections are huge signposts – not letting emotions distort the message on the signpost was my challenge. My experience with this work to date is that if you implement the suggested activities with a desire to make changes, you will come to know so much more about the way you operate and function that you choose to make decisions that work for you, take on challenges you *know* you can achieve, work with people you connect with, and watch your business grow.

Like many things in life, you will get out of this book what you take.

To help you with this journey, there is a Believe in Your Business (BIYB) workbook available to download from www.believeinyourbusiness.info.

'You can't go back and change the beginning, but you can start where you are and change the ending.'

C.S Lewis, British writer, 1898-1963.

Chapter 2

Measures

When doing any type of activity or exercise it helps to measure whether participating has created any change or made you feel any different. The same goes for the exercises in this book. In this chapter you'll create four very different measures. Once you have set them, put them aside until you have completed all the exercises in Chapters 4-9, as you will be revisiting them in Chapter 11.

If you have downloaded the BIYB Workbook from www.believeinyourbusiness.info, turn to the Measures page. If you're not using the workbook, take notes in a convenient way for yourself.

Note: All the activities, exercises and processes in this book are designed to provoke your beliefs or squeeze you to find your lemon juice. To get the most out of each activity, jot down all the thoughts you have – good and not so good – plus any feelings you may experience while working through each section and your actions. If you find yourself making a second cup of tea before you've even started, that's a great sign of resistance. The more thoughts you catch, the more you will discover about yourself. Throughout the workbook there is plenty of space to do this.

Measure 1:
My Eulogy

'If you're going to live, leave a legacy. Make a mark on the world that can't be erased.'

Maya Angelou, civil rights activist, 1928-2014.

Dying is the *only* thing that is guaranteed in this lifetime, so why is it the least talked about subject? Why is it something that is ignored until somebody gets a serious illness or is involved in an accident? Only then do we talk about death and dying as though it's unfair or not right. It's going to happen to *all* of us.

While we are living we have the opportunity to choose our life, where we live, what work we do, who we share our life with, how much money we make, whether we travel – so what does *your* life look like? How do you wish to be remembered when you do die (and very few of us know when that will be)?

This exercise gives you the opportunity to travel ahead in time and write your own eulogy.

This is probably something you have never thought about before and you may find it a little uncomfortable. It is a really significant exercise to use as a gauge.

Either write in the headstone diagram in the BIYB workbook or draw your own headstone shape on a separate sheet of paper and begin with, 'I wish to be remembered … '

I have chosen this exercise for two reasons. Firstly, because it shows immediately whether you are heading in that direction – so, if you died in the next couple of months would your eulogy read true? And secondly, when making future decisions you can see whether your choices are bringing you closer to achieving your eulogy or taking you further from it.

> *Know your lemon juice: This is a good time to make a note of the thoughts going through your mind. Jot down anything and everything you are thinking, whether it makes sense or not.*

Here's an example of John's eulogy:

> 'I wish to be remembered … as a philanthropist and an active member of our community. A compassionate family man and a good husband.'

Here's why John wrote that eulogy:

John wants to donate money and raise money in the community to build a specially adapted bicycle for young children with physical disabilities. He has an engineering background and (before he got married) loved to build things. He watched a documentary once and decided that he would design and build special bicycles and give them to children via an organisation he had heard of.

Here's what John's life currently looks like:

He has a full-time job, a new spouse, two children from his first marriage and a baby on the way. They are a very busy family with work, children's after school activities, weekend sports, preparing for a new baby, etc. There is very little time to do any work on the bike design or to find an organisation to distribute them.

How this exercise helped John:

Putting down on paper – or setting something in stone (literally) – creates an impact. John sees he is currently nowhere near achieving his desire of helping young children with physical disabilities. He doesn't have the time needed to design the bike(s), research for materials and a manufacturer, and find an organisation to donate them to, etc.

How John's eulogy changed his perspective:

What John realises is that he can actually become a philanthropist today – there are many ways he can help others now. This leads to him making a monthly donation to an organisation and finding the time to volunteer with a local environmental community group that his whole family can be part of. He doesn't have to wait until he has designed a bike to be philanthropic.

Hopefully from reading John's eulogy example, you can see the benefit of this exercise. You may need to spend some time reflecting on this or it may come to you immediately. Once you have completed your eulogy put it to one side and move on to the second measure.

Measure 2
My Business Comfort Zone (BCZ)

> *'In any given moment we have two options: To step forward into growth or to step back into safety.'*
>
> Abraham Maslow, American psychologist, 1908 – 1970.

There is a business comfort zone template in the BIYB workbook that you can use or you can draw your own on a separate sheet of paper using the following diagram.

The BCZ wheel is divided into ten segments relating to different components of a business. You may wish to change some of the headings to suit your business or your business comfort zone may have less or more than ten segments.

Focusing on each heading separately, make a few notes about each segment prior to scoring it. What is your immediate thought when you see the heading? There is space in the workbook to make notes.

> *Know your lemon juice: This is where you will catch your true thoughts (beliefs) about that area of your business.*

Areas:

- Bookkeeping/invoicing systems

- Marketing and PR

- Client relationships

- Sales

- All things staff

- Expansion/growth/planning/strategy

- New business

- Management

- Administration/paperwork

- Income/profit

Measures

Once you have made a few notes about each area of your business, mark in each segment on the wheel how you feel that area scores. Each segment of the business comfort zone is marked with a dotted line reflecting the numbers two, four, six, eight and ten. Below the diagram is a scoring guide.

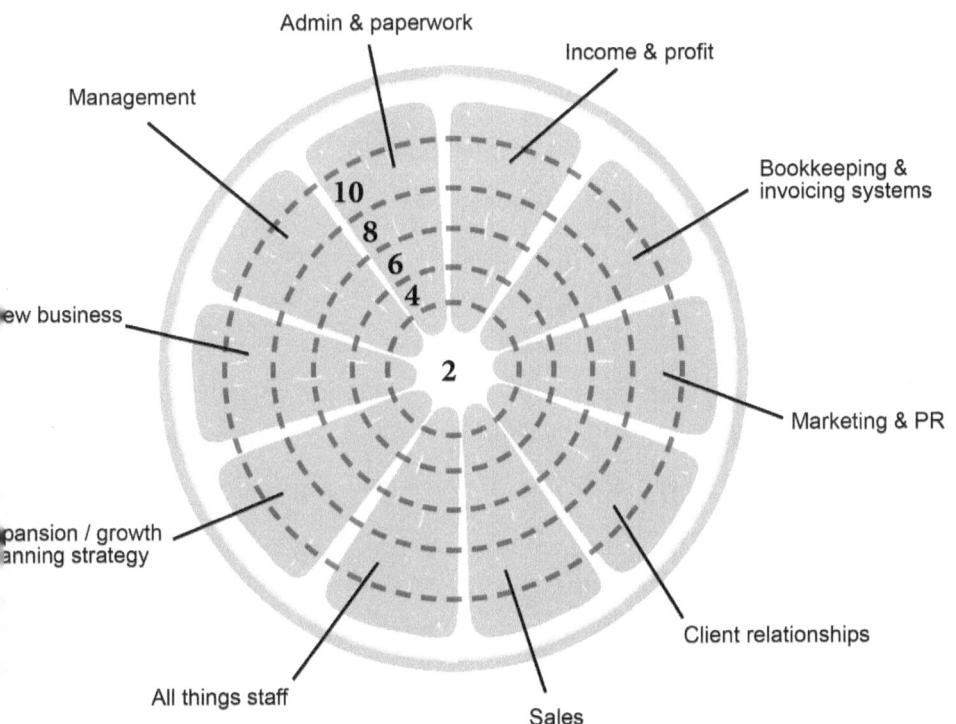

Scoring guide:

- 0-2: This area of my business is on autopilot; I don't invest any effort into this (I want to change it).

- 2-4: This area of my business is OK; it seems to tick along, not improving (this area could be better).

- 4-6: This area of my business is good, running smoothly (I wish to maintain and grow it).

- 6-8: This area of my business is exciting!

- 8-10: I love this area of my business; it's stimulating (it's ready to move to the next level).

The BCZ measure is giving you the opportunity to see the shape of your business (literally). Ideally all segments will be at around the same score and in balance with each other. If your scores are very different, great, that's the purpose of the exercise – to bring all areas into alignment.

When you have completed the scoring process, take the two lowest scoring areas and write a paragraph or statement for each area outlining *ideally* how you would like these areas to be.

Here's an example:

Sue has scored her bookkeeping/invoicing segment 0-2.

> *It's a job she really doesn't enjoy, to the point where anything to do with invoicing and money is put off for as long as possible. When she has to do it, she does it reluctantly and it takes a long time. She doesn't have the money to pay for a bookkeeper, hasn't got the time to find one and is too embarrassed to get one as her accounts are such a mess.*

Sue writes a statement on how *ideally* she would like this segment of her business to be.

> *'Every month a local bookkeeper comes to my office and updates my bookkeeping, pays any bills, sends out any invoices and chases any outstanding invoices. It takes the bookkeeper around one to two hours to keep the money side of my business in order. If there is anything I need to be aware of or if I want to purchase anything for the business, we discuss it. I understand the importance of bookkeeping now and although I don't wish to do it, I certainly understand it. It is worth investing the extra payment each month for peace of mind.'*

Currently, this seems impossible for Sue.

Once you have written your statement(s), put it to one side and leave it until you have completed all the exercises in the rest of the book. If you feel inclined, you could write a statement for all ten segments of your business, as each one will highlight areas for improvement.

Measure 3
I Love You

'What we fear of doing most is usually what we most need to do.'

Ralph Waldo Emerson, philosopher, 1803 – 1882.

For this exercise you will need your mobile phone. Select the camera setting on your phone and switch it so you can see yourself, press the video record button and, looking at yourself, say the following statement:

'[Your name], I love you and I accept you exactly as you are.'

> *Know your lemon juice: At this point jot down how you are feeling and the thoughts that are going through your head.*

You may find this quite confronting because it is possibly not something you have ever done before. Do what you can. If you can't look at yourself and say it, record it anyway. If you can look at yourself but can't say love, say like instead.

The reason I have asked you to record this is so you can look back at it later and see how, by completing the exercises in the book, your thoughts around some things have changed.

If you do not have access to a mobile phone you can do this exercise looking into a mirror.

Why is this exercise relevant to your business? Many aspects of business, especially running your own business, are dependent on building relationships. If *you* don't like yourself very much, why should anyone else like you? If you love yourself, not in an arrogant, pretentious way but in a way that gives you confidence and a genuine presence, people are more likely to warm to you and want to be associated with you. You can practise doing this exercise each day, and each day you will feel more comfortable … I promise.

Measure 4
My One Day List

> *'One day you will wake up and there won't be any more time to do the things you've always wanted. Do it now.'*
>
> Paulo Coelho, Brazilian lyricist and author of The Alchemist, born 1947.

This measure is simply to write your 'one day' list. You know, those things you say you will do one day, and as we know one day is not a day of the week. Next to each desire put a time that you *currently* hope to achieve them by. My sister marks a day each month on her calendar that becomes a 'one day' day – on that day she does something from her list. It's similar to a bucket list.

> *Know your lemon juice: Be aware of what you are saying to yourself when you are making this list and jot down those thoughts.*

At this point, you should have four completed measures, plus a list of thoughts and feelings that came up whilst completing them. In the next chapter, Identifying Your Beliefs, I have outlined a process to discover the underlying beliefs behind your thoughts and feelings.

Put all four measures aside and continue through the chapters. You will revisit your measures in Chapter 11 and discover whether you feel differently about any or all of them.

'Beliefs are what divide people. Doubt unites them.'

Peter Ustinov, English actor, writer and filmmaker,

1921 – 2004.

Chapter 3

Identifying Your Beliefs

Before you begin to identify or recognise your beliefs, this chapter outlines what a belief is, the (basic) science behind a belief, where beliefs come from and why you have different beliefs to a close friend, partner or family member.

What is a belief?

A belief is a thought that you keep thinking until it becomes real or true to you. Your subconscious mind then continues to keep that belief true.

Generally, people operate on autopilot for most of their day – they get out of bed, have a shower, get dressed and have breakfast without *consciously* thinking about what they're doing, unaware of what beliefs they carry. Autopilot is not a bad thing as it enables us to multitask easily. Each time we get behind the wheel of a car we don't have to re-learn how to drive; our subconscious mind has stored that information and recalls how to drive. The more often we carry out an activity the less we have to consciously think about how to do it.

By becoming aware of what we believe we begin to see why life is as it is and, if we want to, we can change things.

A very simple example of a thought becoming a belief would be you thinking (or saying) to yourself, *I'm so clumsy* every time you drop something or make a mistake. Having heard this a few times, your subconscious mind accepts this as real and continues to make sure you keep being clumsy. Before you realise it, *I'm so clumsy* becomes true to you.

The thought *I'm so clumsy* has now become a belief. Once you create a belief, your subconscious mind, as a way of helping you, reminds you of your belief at every opportune moment. As you pick up an expensive item in a store, you hear that voice in your head say, 'I'm so clumsy,' and you put the item down quickly. You also begin to pre-empt the belief. As you are about to be handed a platter of food to take to guests at the table, you say out loud, 'Don't give that to me. I'm so clumsy, I'll probably drop it,' and so the reinforcement of the belief strengthens.

Over time the fact that you have *become* clumsy will start to have greater implications. Your friends and family will notice and start to confirm your clumsiness and they may avoid asking you to do certain things as they, too, now see you as clumsy. You begin to doubt yourself and your own abilities and turn down an invitation to go to dance lessons with a friend, as you assume you will be clumsy at that, too. The belief is now well and truly real to you and begins to impact your life.

This could be perceived as a light-hearted example, however, it shows how easily what we think and say to ourselves can become true and impact the way we live – often without us realising it.

The (very basic) science behind a belief

There are many people whose work has influenced my journey of learning about the belief system, particularly Dr Joe Dispenza, Dr Bruce H Lipton and Dr Wayne Dyer. Dispenza and Lipton are scientists who are disrupting conventional science by proving two major findings: *thought alone can change your body* and *thought alone can change your brain*. These new sciences within quantum mechanics are known as epigenetics and neuroplasticity, respectively.

Epigenetics

Simply put, genetics is what makes us who we are. It is the study of inherited characteristics or genes. Epigenetics

– originally coined in the 1950s – when broken down, literally means on top of genes, and is the study of genes in different environments or gene *expression*. Epigenetics is what controls our genes because it turns certain genes on (becoming active) and off (becoming dormant), depending on our environmental influences. Here are a few influences that can affect our genes: nature, diet, how much and what types of exercise we do, where we live, the people we interact with, parenting, where we sleep, aging, smoking, drinking and air pollution – to list just a few.

So, is it nature or nurture that influences who you become? The power of believing something (your internal environment) influences the outcome. The following excerpt is from Gregg Braden's *The Spontaneous Healing of Belief,* published in 2008.

> *'The famous Framingham Heart Study, initiated under the direction of the National Heart Institute (now known as the National Heart, Lung, and Blood Institute – NHLBI) in 1948, documented the power of just such an effect. The study began with 5,209 men and women, all from Framingham, Massachusetts, who were between the ages of 30 and 62. The purpose of the research was to follow a cross section of people over a long period of time to identify the then-unknown factors of heart disease. In 1971 the program initiated a second study based on the children of the original group, and the research has now begun to recruit a third group, composed of the grandchildren of*

the original subjects. Every two years, the participants are evaluated for the risk factors that have been identified throughout the study. Although the study group represents a broad cross section of people from a variety of lifestyles, the discovery that the participants' belief played a role in their risk for heart disease was surprising to the researchers. Of the many statistics drawn from the study, correlations showed that women who believed they were prone to heart disease were nearly four times as likely to die as those with similar risk factors who didn't hold this belief.'

When it comes to nurture, the environment you are born into (your external environment), you may be born with a capacity to be tall and confident, but if you are undernourished and abused as a child, you are likely to turn into a stunted and fearful adult instead.

These two examples show that both your internal and external environment literally shape who you become.

Neuroplasticity

Neuroplasticity is the capacity of the brain to act and respond to internal and external changes. It enables billions of nerve cells (neurons) to help in different learning processes through creating or rearranging neural pathways through communication between the nerves.

Neuroplasticity gives us the ability to store a new set of information or to master a new skill.

When you are consciously grateful, you are likely to experience higher flows of reward-related neurotransmitters, like dopamine. There is a scientific process called 'self-directed neuroplasticity'(Church, 2014). This process refers to intentionally shaping the brain through controlled use of attention – focusing on things you choose. If you routinely focus your attention on something you regret, you build a very different neural state in your mind than if you intentionally focus on things that you're grateful and happy about.

The challenging part of this process is having a strong command of where you focus your attention. You live in a world that's so full of distraction it's becoming harder to focus on the way you want things to be and very easy to stay focused on how things currently are. Gaining control over your attention is more crucial now than ever before.

Your Reticular Activating System

Each of us sees the world in our own unique way due to a number of factors, some being how we were raised, the religion and traditions our family practise, experiences we've had, situations we've witnessed, the style of education we received, the relationships we've experienced, our chosen lifestyle, the books we read, and so on. Once we establish what we believe and settle into our life, we build on what we know – we live by and defend our beliefs and why shouldn't we? We can prove that what we believe is true most of the time. Herein lies the reason we all see the world in our own unique way – we each have our own filter that we personally feed information to.

At the top of the spinal column there's a piece of the brain called the Reticular Activating System (RAS). It's about two inches long and the width of a pencil, wired to all our senses (except smell) acting as a filter or gatekeeper for all the sensory information we encounter daily.

Your RAS takes what you focus on and creates a filter for it. It then sifts through the data and presents only the pieces of information that are important and relevant to you as a result of what you believe. The RAS programs itself to work in your favor without you noticing it or actively doing anything.

In the same way, the RAS seeks information that validates your beliefs – hence they become real or true to you. It filters the world through the parameters you give it and your beliefs shape those parameters. If you think you are bad at giving speeches, you probably will be (*Message from the Dean*, 2018). If you believe you work efficiently, you most likely do.

Your RAS helps you see what you want to see and in doing so influences your actions and shapes your life. Your RAS also keeps you in your comfort zone, a safe and familiar place that feels comfortable. This is why so many people perceive change as hard or scary because it is uncomfortable and unfamiliar and what we often call *wrong*.

Below is an interpretation of why for the majority of people nothing much changes in twenty-four hours. Unless we change one of the 50-70,000 thoughts we have each day, our lives will remain as they are and won't ever change.

Why nothing much changes in twenty-four hours:

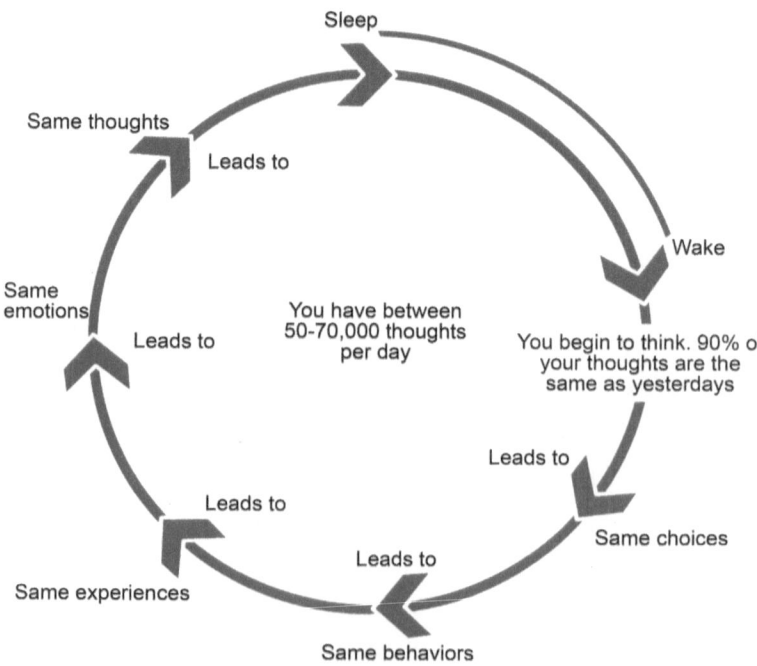

It's only possible to change a thought if you know what you are thinking.

Many books have been written about how powerful our thoughts are. You can find some listed in the additional reading section at the end of this book.

Where do your beliefs come from?

Initially beliefs are given to you or picked up by you.

The moment you arrive on this planet as a newborn baby your empty mind begins to pick up information, firstly through the energy of the environment you're in, the feeling from your carers, noises that are calming and sounds that are upsetting. As you grow you begin to observe the behaviours of those around you and, once you are able to communicate, you absorb and retain *everything* you see and hear and are told. By the age of seven, research shows that your empty mind is now full and your personality has been formed (*Happy Healthy Child: A Holistic Approach*, 2012).

This concept has been around for centuries with Francis Xavier (1506-1552), a missionary and co-founder of the Society of Jesus (also known as the Jesuits), credited with stating, 'Give me the child until he is seven and I will show you the man.'

If you never questioned the information you absorbed in those first few years, the set of beliefs, which become your values, will be the basis on which you make all future decisions and, in turn, will create your behaviours and therefore shape your life.

The influencing by our elders continues through primary and secondary schooling and further education institutions. All these messages are another's perception, not your own. Even in the first job you get there are boundaries and expectations outlined by the company employing you.

These influences continue to be reinforced by your circle of friends, peers, local community, the media and society in general. Because no two people have identical life experiences you have different beliefs from your close friends, partner and even family members.

The common thread with all of these influences is they are keeping you safe and making sure you fit in to your environment and society. These influences could also be perceived as programming or controlling. Your carers have a need to control you and keep you safe as a child; schools and education institutions have hundreds of children to control and keep safe.

A business has a reputation to protect so needs to ensure its employees fit in to and reflect its perceived image.

You can reference your own views here regarding governments controlling populations.

As you get older you will defend your beliefs, often to keep yourself feeling safe – in your comfort zone – in order to keep the life you have created from changing. This is not right or wrong; it's an observation that highlights we are *not* encouraged or naturally given the opportunity to discover our *own* beliefs.

Unfortunately, it's often not until something major happens – illness, divorce, death of a loved one, redundancy – that you reflect back on your life and have a realisation that you are not really doing what you always wanted to do. Remember that question you were asked at school: 'What do you want to be when you grow up?' What was your answer? A doctor or dancer? In my case it was a window dresser and fashion designer.

Have you fulfilled your childhood dreams? Did you forget that desire because life took over and now you feel too old to follow that dream? Before we took on everyone else's well-meaning beliefs we had a set of our own desires and dreams, ready to grow with us – but somehow they got lost along the way.

What's 'wrong' with your beliefs?

There is absolutely nothing *wrong* with the beliefs you have and they have definitely served you to this point and may well continue to. However, the fact you are reading this book is an indication that you possibly want to make some changes in your business or work life and these pages offer a way for you to explore that.

Beliefs reflect *everything* you do – from the way you stand, dress and deal with stress to what you contribute to a meeting and the way you speak.

If you dig deep into a simple thing like how you dress, you will discover *why* you dress like you do. It could result in any number of findings, possibly one of the following: 'My dad always wore a tie to work,' (so you believe it's the right way to dress); 'I wear designer clothes because they make me look more attractive,' (a belief that you are not good enough); 'If I wear this I won't stand out too much,' (a belief that it's not good to be seen); 'Everyone in this industry dresses like this,' (a belief that you need to fit in); 'If I dress like this I will be considered more professional,' (a belief that you are not professional enough). Behind every behaviour there is a reason *why* and that reason stems from a belief.

Your beliefs are restricting your perspective

I like to use the analogy of boulders in a flowing river, the water representing your energy levels, the boulders your beliefs.

A slow, meandering river could represent a person who is happy as they are, doesn't take risks and lives a similar life day in, day out. A raging river, suitable for white water rafting, could represent a person who is so busy and scattered and stressed that they are almost incapable of resting. The boulders in these rivers dictate the flow of the water.

A meandering river may not have many boulders creating rapids but they will be creating the slow flow guiding the water in certain directions preventing it from gathering too much momentum.

The positioning of the boulders in the rapid river will look less strategically placed, appearing to cause a struggle between the water and its obstacles. By removing boulders from either river, the water flow will change.

By removing a belief, you too, will allow your energy to flow in a different way, creating a new perspective and the opportunity to change.

Example of how a belief disrupts your energy flow

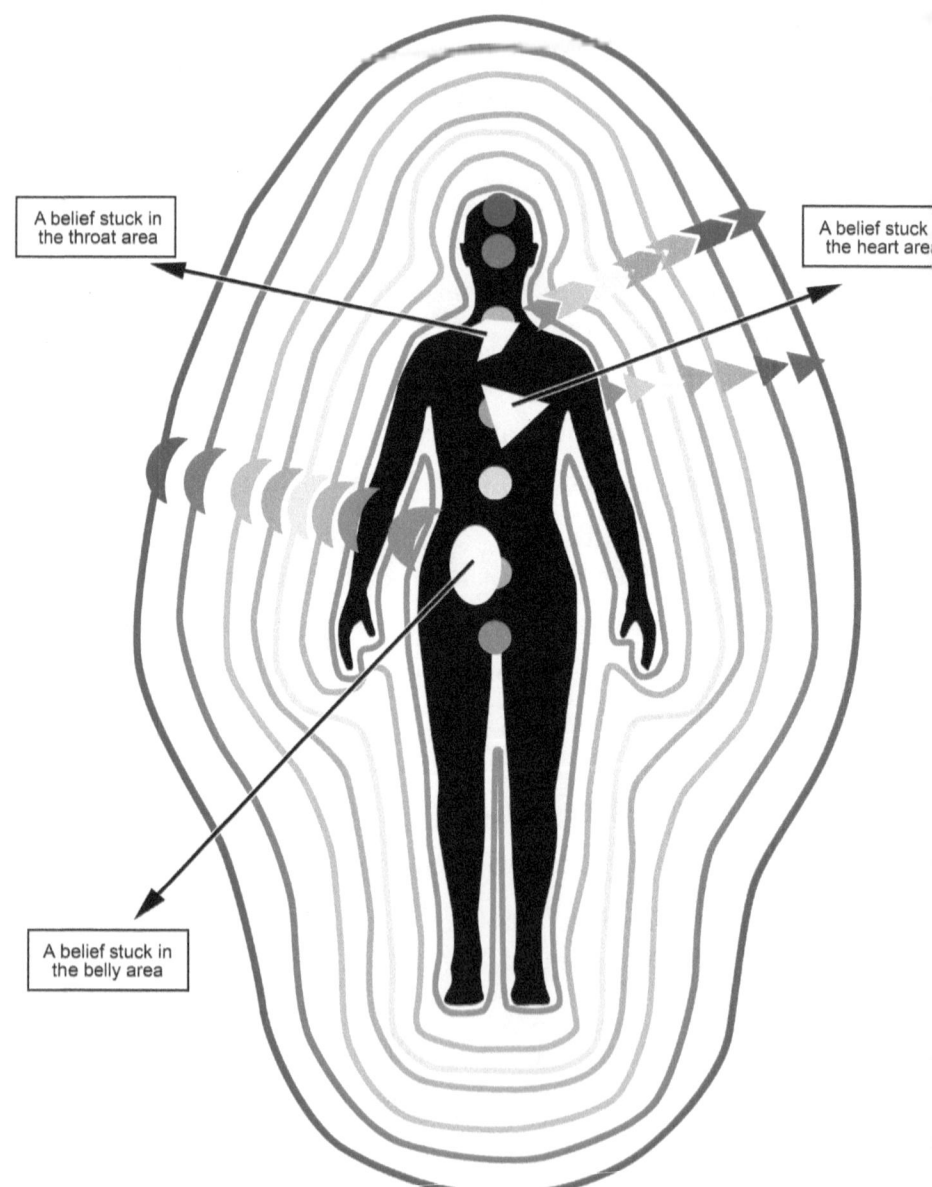

Recognising your beliefs

In order for you to recognise a belief, knowing what's going on in your mind is crucial and this begins with monitoring or observing your daily thoughts. As mentioned earlier, it is said we have between 50,000-70,000 thoughts per day, 80% of which are negative and most of which we had the previous day, so managing them could be perceived as a full-time job in itself. The important thing to understand is that it is possible and a small-steps approach is the best way to start.

Being aware of what you are thinking at certain times of the day is a good place to begin. For example, when you wake up, what is your first thought? When you are cleaning your teeth, what are you thinking about? When traveling to work or to see a client, what are you thinking? This may sound like a strange thing to ask. You probably believe that when you're cleaning your teeth that that's what you're thinking about. If you are, fantastic! That shows you are present. However, 99.999% of people are not thinking about the task they are doing – they are either thinking about something in the past or something in the future and are operating on autopilot.

By focusing on the task at hand you will eliminate any random thoughts (well, most of them) and bring your mind into the present moment.

This is the only time you have any control, in the present moment, and this is where and when you make *conscious* decisions as opposed to subconscious or autopilot decisions.

The majority of the population across the globe is living in a state referred to as unconscious, also known as *automatic pilot* or *programmed*. When a person is not present (unconscious) they are usually in one of two other states.

They are either *worried* because they are thinking about (and living in) the past or *anxious* because they are thinking about (and living in) the future, both of which impact their present situation. What's in the past is exactly that and what may or may not transpire in the future cannot be managed or controlled until you are actually there. So, as you can see, observing your thoughts is not a natural behaviour (yet).

You will recognise your beliefs when you become aware of what you are thinking.

You have your list of thoughts, now what?

Once you have caught the thoughts that were running through your head, the next stage is to explore *why* you had that thought and what *belief* it is coming from.

Identifying Your Beliefs

You may find that you have a number of thoughts that stem from just one core belief.

Below is an example of how to find the *beliefs* underlying these common thoughts and feelings.

I am using the example of the expensive sports car as this never fails to provoke a comment.

When a beautifully designed, expensive sports car travels down the street, every person who notices it will have a thought rush through their mind.

With each thought there will be a corresponding feeling (there will have been a physical action too, but for this exercise we are looking at the thought and feeling only).

The feeling is the clue to the belief behind the thought.

The next stage is to ask why it invoked that feeling, especially if it was a negative one. The examples on the following page should help you see the association.

Thought	Feeling	Examples
Look at them showing off	Jealousy	Their belief could be *I'll never be able to afford such a beautiful car*, so their subconscious mind keeps that belief true by thinking something negative towards a person who can afford such a beautiful car.
Wow, wish I could afford one of those	Lack	Their belief could be *only rich people have cars like that, I'll never be rich*, so their subconscious mind keeps that belief true with a negative thought, and they are unable to see the situation any differently.
Wow, can't wait to have one of those	Optimism	The belief could be *I know I will have one of those one day*, so their subconscious mind keeps the belief true with a positive thought and feeling of hope.
Hmm, bet I know what s/he does for a living	Suspicion	The belief could be *they must have done something illegal to afford to buy that car*, so their subconscious mind keeps the belief true with a disapproving thought.
Hmm, wonder what s/he does for a living	Intrigue	The belief could be *it's good to see people enjoying the rewards of their work*, so their subconscious mind keeps this belief true with a thought of positivity.
Bet her sugar daddy bought her that	Judgement	The belief could be *women can't earn enough to buy a car like that*, so their subconscious mind keeps this belief true with a derogatory thought.

What does this have to do with your business?

How does an example about a car impact your business? If you can (even hypothetically) identify with one of the above thoughts, it shows you have a hidden belief. If the underlying belief that was identified from this example was jealousy, lack, suspicion or judgment it shows two things. Firstly, this is your lemon juice – it came from within you. Secondly, that belief is probably not restricted to seeing an expensive car. It is safe to say, if you hold that belief, it will in some way be impacting *all* areas of your life including your business.

Let's use Example 2: feeling poor. The underlying belief was *I'll never be rich* (although the example is reflecting financially rich, the belief potentially could keep you feeling lack in other areas). If this is your belief – *I'll never be rich* – then your subconscious mind will go all out to ensure that remains your truth. When running a business, that's the last hidden obstacle you want in your way.

Exploring your own thoughts

This process can lead you down a rabbit hole, which is great because from a simple thought you may discover a significant belief that, once removed, makes way for huge growth. When you have your list of thoughts, take each one and examine it. You'll need to ask yourself some questions to find the belief behind the thought. After a while you will begin to see immediately where the thought came from, what triggered it and whether you wish to keep thinking that way.

Start with these questions, designed to explore a thought and find the belief. Some questions may appear irrelevant, while others will hit the nail on the head. As soon as you recognise the underlying belief, write it down and move to the next thought.

Why did I think that?

What was I feeling when I said that?

What triggered me to think that?

Is that really what I think?

Is that thought true to me?

Who did that thought come from?

Do others in my family think that?

Is this thought serving me?

How would I feel if I didn't think this?

Is this thought protecting me?

Is this thought aligned with who I truly am?

Can I live without this thought?

What belief is this thought linked to?

Remember, some of your beliefs could have been lying dormant for years. When you have identified the *belief* that the thought stems from, create a separate list of your beliefs only.

The final stage is to take the newly discovered beliefs that you can now see are no longer serving you and remove them using one of the unique techniques outlined in Chapter 10.

Finding your beliefs

In addition to observing your own thoughts as you go about your daily business, you can also choose to look for beliefs relating to specific areas of your life. I've chosen six topics relevant to growing your business and they are presented in the following G.R.O.W.T.H chapters. I encourage you to make a note of your thoughts, your actions and how you feel while reading about each topic and when carrying out the associated exercises. Discovering what you are feeling or thinking is the *lemon juice* you are looking for to help you move forward.

When approaching the exercises and processes you might think, *This doesn't apply to me* or *I don't need to do this particular exercise*. I suggest you do the exercise regardless, because what could be happening is your subconscious mind doesn't want you to delve into that particular subject/exercise as it could take you out of your comfort zone and cause you to disrupt a currently comfortable situation. When we feel resistance towards something it usually indicates we need to go there.

Be prepared to get comfortable with being uncomfortable and tasting your lemon juice.

'A winner is a dreamer who never gives up.'

Nelson Mandela, South African anti-apartheid revolutionary, 1918 – 2013.

G
= Ground Work

Chapter 4
Laying Your Own Foundations

Are your strengths really your strengths or are they labels you have grown into?

When I was in my early teens, I was known within my family as Gaynor the Entertainer, but not because I could sing and dance or perform on demand for my family to show off their talented daughter. No, that label came from a passing comment by a family friend, because I had a natural ability to make people laugh. I carried the *I am funny* label with pride for many years, and it was true: I could make people laugh and I liked that people thought that about me.

Fast-forward twenty-five years. I attended a weekend workshop exploring archetypes. Swiss psychiatrist Carl

Jung introduced the concept of archetypes. Jung believed that archetypes were models of people, behaviours, or personalities. Archetypes, he suggested, were inborn tendencies that play a role in influencing human behaviour.

In the workshop, we had to select an archetype we believed we embodied with the intention of exploring it. Easy. I chose the Joker. Within minutes of making my selection I had tears of sadness pouring down my face and my chest became tight as I saw clearly for the first time why I made people laugh when I was younger.

I lived with both my parents and my younger brother and sister. My older sister had left home to study and travel when I was about twelve years old. My father was a gentle man, kind, caring and loved by many. As a child my perception of my mother was that she was in charge and at times I was scared of her. Being scared of a parent significantly shaped who I became. I could sense when she wasn't happy and I learnt ways to make her and others laugh to change the atmosphere.

My experience at the archetype workshop when I focused on the Joker revealed that role as being a form of protection, a mask, an easy way to deal with a not-so-easy situation, a façade that I hid my true self behind for far too long. As for it being a strength, it started out as a label, however, I still list *I am funny* as one of my top ten strengths. Now I own it and know that I'm not hiding behind it because I do think I'm funny!

The beliefs I formed from my home environment as a result of this became my double-edged sword. The good that came from this experience was my resilience, an ability to read people's moods, sensitivity to energy and, most significantly, my resourcefulness, for which I am truly grateful.

The more burdening beliefs I formed were that it was my role to rescue everyone, or at least make them feel included, whether they wanted to be or not. I also mastered the art of keeping people from getting close to me, because a belief had formed that it wasn't safe to let people I loved too close. That has been a heavy weight to carry.

I was unaware of these beliefs that had shaped my life so significantly until I was in my early forties. This was also the time I became a mum, which caused some of my awareness. Looking back, I can now see clearly how my beliefs became the foundation for many decisions I made and how they played out and shaped my reality, influencing all areas of my life, including my approach to business.

When building anything – a house, a team, or a business – a strong foundation is essential for its stability as it grows. As a business owner or business leader, you play a huge part in the quality of your business or team's foundation. This chapter gives you the opportunity to reassess what it is you bring to the business: your attributes, qualities, skills and experience all packaged neatly as your *strengths*.

We've created a simple way for you to dig a little deeper and update or refresh your strengths list by looking at them from a slightly different perspective. When it comes to strengths it's easy to create a list of talents and skills that have served you well so far. This list of strengths is often followed by a request for a list of your weaknesses, too. Not here. We are only interested in you owning your strengths, not correcting your weaknesses. In particular, we want to help you discover your *signature* strengths.

What is a signature strength?

A signature strength is a strength that best reflects who you truly are. It often shows your values, too. It is a strength that you own, you are proud of, one that serves you, a strength you can incorporate into your daily life and one you can speak about and share with pride.

Shawn Achor, author of *The Happiness Advantage*, has proved that people feel more positive and are more productive after just one week of consciously using their signature strengths.

G = Ground Work

Pre-exercise suggestion: *Prior to beginning any of the exercises, use the BIYB Workbook, which you can download from www.believeinyourbusiness.info, or, if you don't have the workbook, have a piece of paper or notebook available to answer the questions and catch those first, fleeting thoughts and beliefs. You may perceive them as reasons you don't have to do a specific exercise (aka excuses). If that's how they come to you, still jot them down. You could possibly get a feeling like dread or anxiety or even elation or excitement, or you may find yourself physically avoiding the exercise by leaving the room to get another drink. This, too, is vital information: write it down. The more you can capture what is going on in your mind and body when confronted with particular tasks, the more lemon juice you will discover.*

Exercise 1
Listing your strengths

Part 1

Start by writing a list of at least twenty of your strengths. There is space in the BIYB workbook, or do this on a separate piece of paper. List the strengths you have as a male or female, a parent, sibling, son or daughter, as a business owner, an employer, employee, activist, volunteer or athlete. Think of what strengths you have when you are under pressure or stressed, when presenting to a client or pitching for new business. Try to consider all areas of your life and list *every* strength that comes to mind.

> *Know your lemon juice: This is a good time to make a note of the thoughts going through your mind while you are making this list. Jot down anything and everything you are thinking, whether it makes sense or not.*

When listing your strengths, personalise them. If you've written good communicator as a strength, list it as *I am a good communicator*. This helps you to connect to the strength and own it.

Strengths can also be mistaken for labels that we and others use to describe ourselves in order to fit in or get a job or look good. There is a big difference between labelling yourself a good communicator and genuinely *being* a good communicator. If it is a label, people will have trouble seeing that strength in you. Sure, it's listed on your CV or personal profile, but if it's not a trait or quality that is natural to you it won't ring true to others. If, however, you believe with unwavering certainty that you are a good communicator, it will be seen and experienced by everyone who meets you.

Part 2

When you have compiled your list, explore each strength individually to discover whether you actually own it. By exploring your list of strengths you will begin to see which ones are your innate qualities and which are just labels you've picked up along the way. Knowing which strengths are genuine then gives you the opportunity to harness them and use them to your advantage.

To do this there are some questions listed for you to use to unpack each strength. These questions are in the BIYB workbook or you can re-write them from the example below. Here is an example using the questions to show you what could happen:

Example:

Sarah has written *I am a good communicator* as one of her strengths. Using the questions to unpack that strength this is what she discovers:

Q: Have you always been ... a good communicator?
A: *I think so. People always say I'm good at talking to people.*

Q: When did you first realise you were ... a good communicator?
A: *When I worked for XXXX five years ago.*

Q: When you think about that strength how do you feel?
A: *Personally, I feel I am better at writing than talking.*

Q: Do you believe you are ... a good communicator?
A: *Yes, I do, but I communicate best through my books.*

Q: Does this strength serve you in your work life and/or your personal life?
A: *Mainly work life.*

Q: Do you think this strength could be broken down into other strengths, either in addition to or instead of ... good communicator?

A: *Definitely. I am a published author, I am a good writer, I am good with words … these all sound better to me.*

Q: Would you be happy to stand up and introduce yourself as … a good communicator?
A: *Not really, I rarely call myself that!*

Q: If not, what name do you give the strength or strengths instead?
A: *I'd prefer to use one of the new strengths from a previous question. I am a published author, I am a good writer, and I am good with words.*

Although that is a brief example, it highlights a couple of things.

1. When we are *known* for being a certain way and we hear people describe us that way, we often take on that label and call it a strength.
2. Sometimes a strength could be too broad, so try to be as precise as possible.
3. When a strength is only applicable to one aspect of your life, take a closer look at it – your strengths are part of your whole life.
4. Don't say you are something you're not – a label doesn't serve you.
5. When you feel you can stand up and acknowledge that strength to others, you know it's yours and you own it.

It's beneficial to do this process with a trusted friend, mentor or work colleague, with the aim being to convince them that you own each of your strengths. Both of you could make a list of strengths and take it in turns to ask each other the questions – until you both feel comfortable with the final list. If you prefer, you can do the exercise by yourself. The gold lies in your honesty.

Part 3

The final part of this exercise is to recognise your top three strengths or your *signature strengths*. These are the ones that most resonate with you, that best describe you, and that you own with unwavering certainty.

If you have the opportunity to speak in a group environment try to incorporate your strengths into your introduction or talk, if appropriate. Mention them when you are talking to clients or potential clients, let people know that's what you're good at, that's what you do best, and that these are the strengths that make you, you.

Exercise 2

Owning your signature strengths

Rewrite your verbal branding, your introduction, to reflect at least two of your three newly identified signature strengths, then get used to describing yourself in this way. Saying it out loud the first few times is not as easy as saying it in your head, so get comfortable with confidently delivering it.

There is a space in the BIYB workbook for this exercise.

Exercise 3
Implementing your signature strengths

Now that you are feeling confident about the foundations you are laying for yourself and therefore your business or team, list the areas of your business/work where you can see your signature strengths creating impact and begin to use them daily.

Post-exercise suggestion: *On completion of the exercises you will have a list of beliefs, thoughts, feelings and actions around this particular topic that you are now consciously aware of. Your objective is to discover the underlying belief(s). If you are not sure what the belief is, you can go back to the section called Exploring Your Own Thoughts in Chapter 3 to explore the thought some more. Once you have a list of beliefs you can choose to manage, change or remove them. How to do this is outlined in Chapter 10.*

'Everyone at some point in life has faced rejection and failure, it is part of the process to self-realisation.'

Lailah Gifty Akita Ghanaian, author and founder of Smart Youth Volunteer Foundation.

R
= Rejection

Chapter 5
Bouncing Back

If you only choose to read one chapter of this book (although I hope you don't) make it this one. Rejection comes in many forms and can be paralysing. It comes as a gift – wrapped in toilet paper. Yes, rejection is a gift. The reason it comes wrapped in toilet paper is because you don't always see it as a gift when you first receive it.

The definition of the verb reject is to refuse to accept, and to discard as useless or unsatisfactory. The act of rejection invariably stirs the emotion of disappointment. This chapter offers you ways to manage your disappointment to enable you to keep on track until you have the space to clear the belief(s) the emotion is connected to.

My own journey with rejection began almost twenty-five years ago. I knew from the moment my feet touched the tarmac at Perth airport on my very first visit to Australia in 1994 that I was *meant* to live here. I felt an indescribable, deep connection that I still cannot put into words. I somehow just knew and that knowing kept me hopeful for eight long years. During those eight years, I visited three times on holiday visas, searching for the opportunity to be here permanently, including trying to find a business to sponsor me. I hired an immigration lawyer to find a way for me to get a visa and on two occasions she was successful, only to be notified shortly after that the government had amended the law yet again. At the end of each of those trips I relived the rejection and the disappointment of having to leave, no closer to living there than when I arrived.

During my first trip I took a job with an independent events company. The owner and I worked well together and when I expressed my desire to live in Australia permanently he agreed to look into sponsoring me.

The wheels were in motion. Part way through the application in late 1995 I got news from home that my father had been diagnosed with late stage bone cancer and, although nobody would say how long he would live, it was obvious he was not going to survive. I travelled back to the UK, with a blessing from my boss.

R = Rejection

Three months after arriving home, with every intention of returning to my job in Australia, I received a letter from the owner of the business. It outlined that the application was going through successfully and that he was excited that I would be part of the development of his business moving forward. The final part of the letter, however, was an ultimatum. He would only continue with the sponsorship if I returned to Australia within one month from the date of the letter. What a dilemma: spend the final days, weeks, months with my father and family or return to Australia with the chance of receiving a permanent visa, which I wanted so much.

It was a simple decision. My father died just two months later. I was with him as he announced his departure with his deafening death throes.

My two subsequent trips were spent looking for new potential sponsors, to no avail. After each trip, I would return to the UK, find a job and quietly hope for a miracle. When I returned from my third holiday visa visit I gave up the dream. I bought a house in the UK and settled back into life as I knew it. I got a good job with a company car and I even got a cat – a big sign I was staying put.

There's a long story between me buying that house and buying my final one-way ticket to Australia in January 2002

– maybe it's another book for my daughter to understand the extraordinary synchronicity that unfolded to make sure she came into this world – and in hindsight I can see exactly why the journey took eight years.

All the tears and doubt I experienced from the rejection of not being allowed to stay and having to say goodbye to my Australian friends, some of whom are still my friends twenty-five years later, was all worth it. Moving to Australia any sooner would not have been right. Certain things had to happen in my life and my daughter's father's life in order for us all to come together as we did. Each painful rejection was because something wasn't ready. This experience is one of the greatest gifts I have been given.

I definitely didn't manage the rejections or my emotions very well back then. At times, I was inconsolable with grief, but it taught me to view rejection differently and that's what I hope you can take from this chapter.

Although my story relates to personal rejection, rejection is rejection whatever the situation. Here you will find some strategies to help you deal with rejection immediately, ways to move forward and exercises to encourage you to explore your emotions and beliefs around any possible lingering rejection.

R = Rejection

Founder, CEO, manager or leader: as a human being you are not immune to rejection, nor should you try to be. You may have grown a thicker skin over the years but that's not always enough to keep the emotions at bay. Managing your emotions and preventing them from influencing your behaviour is what this chapter covers.

When we've been rejected, in whatever capacity, and we feel hurt, we can sometimes be hard on ourselves and try to brush it off, however, neuroscience now shows that the brain behaves in exactly the same way when rejected as when you experience physical pain. 'We demonstrate the overlap between social rejection and physical pain in these areas by comparing both conditions in the same individuals using functional MRI [...] These results give new meaning to the idea that rejection hurts. They demonstrate that rejection and physical pain are similar not only in that they are both distressing—they share a common somatosensory representation as well.' This excerpt is from the report 'Social rejection shares somatosensory representations with physical pain', published by Proceedings of the National Academy of Science (PNAS). So, it's OK and natural to feel hurt.

I mentioned above that rejection is a gift. A great way for you to realise this is to look back at a rejection you experienced in the past – maybe you didn't get a job you wanted, or the house you loved, or a relationship didn't go the way you'd hoped. With the luxury of hindsight, you can now see what happened after that particular rejection. I'm guessing you ended up with a better job, house or relationship. It's only when you initially experience the rejection that it doesn't always feel like a gift.

Another reason why a rejection can be perceived as a gift is because your reaction highlights your lemon juice. You get to see what's triggered, what beliefs come to the surface and you have the opportunity to observe the feelings and a chance to change that. The greater your reaction to rejection, the stronger the indication that the underlying belief is not serving you.

If you receive a rejection when you are feeling good, when almost everything in your life is running smoothly – your relationship is better than ever, the business is exceeding targets, you feel healthy and optimistic – the impact will be minimal because you will have a strong sense of yourself and your purpose. It's when you are not feeling good and a rejection hits that the disconnection appears more obvious.

Knowing this now gives you the option to make a choice: let the hurt affect the rest of your day/week/month or find the belief(s) behind the emotion and clear them.

R = Rejection

Listed below are three ways to help you manage rejection and your disappointment on the spot, creating space for you until you are in a position to look more closely at why you felt and/or responded the way you did.

> *Know your lemon juice: This is a good time to make a note of any initial thoughts going through your mind. Jot down anything and everything you are thinking, whether it makes sense or not. Your mind may go back to a time you were rejected in the past, make a note of how that makes you feel now.*

Pre-exercise suggestion : *Prior to beginning any of the exercises, use the BIYB Workbook which you can download from www.believeinyourbusiness.info or, if you don't have the workbook, have a piece of paper or notebook available to answer the questions and catch those first, fleeting thoughts and beliefs. You may perceive them as reasons you don't have to do a specific exercise (aka excuses). If that's how they come to you, still jot them down. You could possibly get a feeling like dread or anxiety or even elation or excitement, or you may find yourself physically avoiding the exercise by leaving the room to get another drink. This, too, is vital information: write it down. The more you can capture about what is going on in your mind and body when confronted with particular tasks, the more lemon juice you will discover.*

Exercise 1
Create a Personal Action Plan or PAP

The first exercise is to create a Personal Action Plan or PAP. This is personalised to suit you, your situation and your life, so I can't tell you what's best for you because I don't know you. What I can do is give you some pointers to help you build your own action plan options. I recommend you include the first two options in your plan and then choose from the remaining six according to what you feel would be most suitable for you.

Option 1:
Stop the knee-jerk reaction (recommended)

It's safe to say that everybody has a knee-jerk reaction to rejection – the way you behave *immediately* after you receive a rejection. This behaviour comprises of three components working simultaneously – a physical *action*, a *thought* and an *emotion* – all in a split second. Your first and possibly greatest challenge of your PAP is to *manage* this behaviour. Typically, this behaviour consists of walking away or storming off, saying something irrelevant, or physically making a statement like thumping the desk. This action often happens automatically and, given time, it is highly likely you will regret doing it.

How can you manage this? You have a split second, literally, to stop your body from reacting to the emotion – pain, humiliation, fear. This will take practice and, depending on how often you face possible rejection, could influence how long it takes you to conquer this first step. If you are in sales you may have created your own way of dealing with rejection, consider these options which focus on managing your feelings, not ignoring them (which you could have become custom to doing).

To be able to manage your immediate behaviour, allow the thoughts to pass through your mind without engaging with them. It's connecting to your thought(s) that creates the other two components – emotion and action. Allowing your thought(s) to pass through your mind without reacting or responding is a learned process. It's been proven that if you don't interact with an emotion (brought on by a thought) it will dissipate. In brain researcher Jill Bolte Taylor's book, *A Brain Scientist's Personal Journey*, Taylor describes the 90-second rule as, 'Once triggered, the chemical released by my brain surges through my body and I have a physiological experience. Within 90 seconds from the initial trigger, the chemical component of my anger has completely dissipated from my blood and my automatic response is over. If, however, I remain angry after those 90 seconds have passed, then it is because I have chosen to let that circuit continue to run.'

This process is the equivalent of gym training: the more you do it the better you will become at it. Eventually, there will come a time when you experience a rejection and that old knee-jerk thought will pass through your mind without you reacting to it.

OK. You know what your thoughts *want* you to do (knee-jerk reaction) but this time you are going to do something *completely* different.

Option 2:
Breathe (recommended)

Yes, *breathe*. Remember, you have a split second to control your behaviour, so you are not going to do *anything* except breathe. Take at least three slow, long breaths – more if possible. Silently and slowly count to ten . What you are doing here is making time for your initial thought(s) to pass through so you do not display a (knee-jerk) reaction. That's it. This breathing space is allowing Option 1 to happen – the thought to pass through you. Slow breathing also reduces the adrenalin that has been released, preparing you for the fight, flight or freeze response.

R = Rejection

As you exhale slowly you are telling your body you are not in any danger.

The steps after this depend on the type of person you are and the situation you are in. Choose the options that resonate with you.

Option 3:

Do nothing

Doing nothing does not actually mean nothing. It means choose to take the rejection and leave the situation – not with an attitude or dramatically. For example, it may be appropriate to say, 'I'd like some time to process this,' or, 'Thank you for your time,' or, 'Can we discuss this tomorrow,' before leaving. If it's over the phone say, 'Would it be possible for me to call you later/tomorrow?' before ending the call. The objective is to remove yourself from the situation as soon as you can. This allows any thoughts and emotions to pass. Making a decision or reacting while your body is full of emotion is not your best option.

Option 4:

Let go of the emotion

Different people respond to rejection in different ways at different times. This comes down to a few factors: their current situation, the circumstances, and the potential impact, among others. If you find yourself full of anger, sadness or anxiety, you will need to let that emotion go so that you can continue with your day. If you are running from meeting to meeting or you are about to give a presentation you need a strategy that can release the initial emotion *immediately*. One option is to use one of the Letting Go of Beliefs exercises outlined in Chapter 10, or find a way to park the emotion until you have time to release it later using one of these strategies.

If you have the time (you don't have to go straight to a meeting), I strongly suggest you do something physical – go for a walk or jog, dance to your favourite song, go to the gym or kick a soccer ball. Do something that physically moves your body. Moving shifts your energy and will help to dissipate any built-up blocks of emotional energy. Some people need to verbally vent so, if you drive, get in the car, put some music on and sing it off! It does need to be released as opposed to suppressed.

Option 5:

Avoid making an emotional decision

The worst time to make a decision is when you are full of emotion. This applies to being excited just as much as being hurt. If a decision is made when you are feeling emotional it will be based on how you are feeling *in that moment*, which is not how you feel most of the time. If you can put twenty-four hours between the situation and any decisions you need to make relating to it, then do. Time will reduce the momentum and intensity of an emotion, giving you a clearer perspective. If you don't have the luxury of twenty-four hours, find at least one hour and take advantage of every minute. Get a pen and paper and start to write down how you're feeling – don't stop writing until you've run out of things to write. It doesn't matter what you write; the purpose is to off-load the emotion triggered by the rejection. Often a rejection links back to a previous (similar) rejection or a previous disappointment and stirs up the emotion around that, too. Writing helps to get some of the thoughts out of your head. When you feel more balanced, you can return to your writing and you'll probably discover some beliefs that you never realised you carried. Now, you can remove them.

Option 6:

Find the positives

When you feel ready, make a list of the positives. Yes, there are some positives! Ask yourself, 'What good is coming from this situation?' then listen to your gut. Even if you can only find one positive in the time you have, that's enough. Now take the positives and focus *only* on them. Keep repeating the positives (regardless of how many negatives your mind is throwing at you). Repeat the positives over and over in your head, or out loud if possible. This process will bring the positives to the forefront of your mind and your negative emotions will begin to ease. This exercise is ideal when you have to make a decision and you have little time. When you have more time consider the negative thoughts that were coming up, find the underlying belief(s) and remove them.

Option 7:
Stand strong

This exercise can help reinstate your confidence. It involves Amy Cuddy's Wonder Woman stance. If you're a guy, don't be put off by the name; it's for men too. Stand in what's known as an open power pose, just like Wonder Woman – hands on hips, shoulders back, legs slightly apart – for two minutes, that's all. Cuddy (2015) has tested this and found that just 120 seconds of standing in this pose will reduce your cortisol hormone (stress hormone) by 11% and your testosterone (confidence hormone) will increase by 16%. These measures apply even when a person is calm.

If you are in your car and cannot stand, put your shoulders back, head up, chest out and feel yourself open. The opposite of this is to be hunched over and closed, where no energy can move around the body and you stay stuck. Amy Cuddy gave one of the most-listened to TED Talks. I've referenced it at the back of the book in the additional reading section – it's definitely worth a watch.

Option 8:
Connect a positive emotion to something tangible

Immediately after a rejection the mind can be hard to control. Having something tangible to hold on to can break that running mind. Firstly, choose something tangible that you carry with you or can begin to carry with you. Maybe a key ring or a piece of jewellery or a pen – something you can carry with you or have access to in your everyday work life.

Focus on a positive emotion, a feeling that gives you strength. It could be feeling empowered, in control or calm. Hold the item (for example, a pen), close your eyes and take yourself to a scenario when you last felt that positive emotion. Really step into it. Picture the scene and feel the emotion while holding the pen. Then project that feeling into the pen, feel the emotion coming down your arm and entering the pen. The objective is to create a trigger effect to your brain so that every time you touch the pen you will feel the emotion you have connected to it. This may take a few attempts, but stick at it, as it will be worth it. This is a great way to break the initial train of thought and emotion connected to rejection.

Creating your own Personal Action Plan (PAP)

When choosing your PAP options you are creating a strategy that will work for *you*. It may or may not include some of the steps listed above – they are suggestions and techniques I use. Whatever you choose, make it a simple and effective way to deal with rejection *immediately*. The options you choose may take a bit of practice before you feel the full benefit of them. That's OK, keep practising them and before you know it you will have a plan to manage rejection.

> *Know your lemon juice: This subject could trigger lots of thoughts connected to any rejections you've had in the past – business related or personal. Jot down anything and everything that comes to mind. It may remind you that you still have a bit of a grudge lurking! You'll get to clear all this in Chapter 10.*

R = Rejection

Exercise 2
Standing in someone else's shoes

This concept is something my business coach, Fiona, introduced to me. It can be used whenever you feel you need an extra bit of confidence or strength. In this instance we will use it to handle rejection. Choose a person you respect and/or admire. It could be someone you know personally or somebody who is successful in their industry. It could be somebody famous or even a character from film or TV. You are choosing somebody whose qualities you admire.

The next time you receive a rejection, stand in *that person's* shoes and consider *what would they do in this situation*? How would *they* handle this? What would *they* say? How would *they* feel? Take on their energy and look at the situation through *their* eyes. Whether this works because you are pretending to be them or because you are removing yourself from the situation doesn't matter – I just know it works! As with most new practices, you may need to try it a couple of times and even try a few different people to see who works best.

When you have chosen your person, you can make a note of the traits or characteristics you like about that person. It may help you to begin forming those traits in yourself.

Exercise 3
Personal declaration

I've put this exercise in this chapter however it is probably relevant to all the G.R.O.W.T.H chapters as its purpose is to immediately improve how you feel about yourself. Having a personal declaration is especially beneficial if you are feeling rejected. A personal declaration is like receiving a well-intended pep talk from your best mate; only you don't need to call your best mate because you have your very own version on hand.

Create a statement – maybe two or three sentences – that highlights your qualities. If you've done the exercises in the previous chapter to discover your signature strengths, you may want to include those.

Example:

I'm only ever sent situations I can handle; I've got this. I'm intelligent, capable and confident; I'll get through this. If this isn't the way, I know something better will happen.

You may want to type it into your phone so that when you need it, it's there.

R = Rejection

Note about rejection

It's important to note that rejection is not personal and can trigger lots of past experiences. Remember: it's a gift. You are managing it so that it doesn't distort the rest of your day/week/month.

Once the emotion has passed and you are back on track, it's crucial to put the rejection in perspective, understand why it happened, without analysing it to death. Behind your reaction to rejection is a belief that holds the key – that is what you're looking for. Accept that it happened (as opposed to ignoring it and going into denial), and this will help you move forward. There is a gift in the rejection somewhere. It may be obvious the next day, it may take a month or longer, but at some point you will be able to turn back and say, 'I'm so glad that happened because now ... '

Post-exercise suggestion: *On completion of the exercises you will have a list of beliefs, thoughts, feelings and actions around this particular topic that you are now consciously aware of. Your objective is to discover the underlying belief(s). If you are not sure what the belief is, you can go back to the section called* Exploring Your Own Thoughts *in Chapter 3 to explore the thought some more. Once you have a list of beliefs, you can choose to manage, change or remove them. How to do this is outlined in Chapter 10.*

It always seems impossible, until it is done.'

Nelson Mandela, South African anti-apartheid revolutionary, 1918 – 2013.

O
= Outcome

Chapter 6
The Road Ahead

As an entrepreneur, business owner or influencer it is vital that *you*, the leader, know the outcome you are aiming for.

Having a clear outcome is something I have heard many people struggle with over the years. Regardless of how experienced they are or established their business is, there are times when their vision appears so far away when compared to where they are currently. I've yet to meet anybody who doesn't have an off-day, or who never loses focus. In today's world of constant distraction and instant gratification we are all likely to question our direction occasionally. Having a place to aim for never really disappears; it's the path leading to it that twists and turns creating the illusion we're off track.

As with everything in life (except death), there is no guarantee that you will reach your outcome, but if you know where you are heading, it will help you to stay focused and to drive you and the business forward. This chapter highlights the significance of aiming for something versus just *hoping* for a good result.

If you are a natural goal setter or someone who has experienced the synchronicities that can unfold when you are focused on a particular outcome, this is a way of fine-tuning your focus. If you know about goals but have never really made a commitment to them, I hope you will find this approach inspiring and feel motivated to start. I choose to call goals intentions because for me it makes the *goal* feel more personal and it's *my intention* to achieve *that outcome* so the intention is mine. I have also found that my client's enthusiasm and focus lasts longer when they use the concepts I have suggested below.

Initially, the suggestions may appear a little challenging and long-winded. It may help to create a *draft* version first, sleep on it and return to it. I say this because on different days we can feel different ways. The worst time to be considering your outcome is when you are not feeling great in yourself. You will probably set the bar low and even talk yourself out

O = Outcome

of what you want. The best time to complete the exercises *in this particular section* is when you are feeling good and things are going well – the challenge then is to feel the need to even do the exercises. We've all had those times when we've just secured a good client or contract and we easily slip into the comfort of *this is it, we're on our way,* until the contract ends.

> *Know your lemon juice: However you are feeling when you consider your outcome, don't forget to jot down in your BIYB workbook the thoughts you have, especially around the possibility of things changing or feeling too big to achieve.*

Pre-exercise suggestion: *Prior to beginning any of the exercises, use the BIYB Workbook, which you can download from www.believeinyourbusiness. info or, if you don't have the workbook, have a piece of paper or notebook available to answer the questions and catch those first, fleeting, thoughts and beliefs. You may perceive them as reasons you don't have to do a specific exercise (aka excuses). If that's how they come to you, still jot them down. You could possibly get a feeling like dread or anxiety or even elation or excitement, or you may find yourself physically avoiding the exercise by leaving the room to get another drink. This, too, is vital information, so write it down. The more you can capture what is going on in your mind and body when confronted with particular tasks, the more lemon juice you will discover.*

Exercise 1
Your Outcome Statement

There are five steps for your outcome statement:

1. Write it
2. Believe it
3. Read and visualise it
4. Take action
5. Future decisions

1. Write it

What does your ideal outcome look like in your mind? For this exercise select one area of your business that you wish was different. It could be a topic from your business comfort zone in the measures chapter earlier. If so, you may have already completed this part of the exercise.

Once you've chosen an area to focus on, write down *exactly* how the situation would look if it were how you ideally want it to be. Let the words pour out; imagine you are telling a friend what it looks like. Let your imagination be free. If there were no logistical challenges, no financial restrictions, no time restraints, what would this part of your business look like?

O = Outcome

Include as much detail as possible: the people you are with, the location, how you are dressed, the car you are driving, how you are feeling, everything. This is called your outcome statement. It may help to begin your outcome statement with, 'It's been two months now since … '. This will help evoke a real feeling that it *is* happening, you're already there and you don't have to think about how it's going to happen.

Taking one component of your business makes this concept easier than writing an outcome statement for your whole business, especially if there are lots of areas you'd like to change. If you are struggling to decide where to start, revisit your business comfort zone and look at each section in more detail. Which of the sections would you like to change first? You can have ten outcome statements, but focus on one at a time.

Once you are familiar with this exercise and if the business is going well, an outcome statement for your *whole* business is something you may wish to write. If things are failing in a couple of areas and overall not looking good, an outcome statement for the whole business could be hard to believe and achieve and therefore defeat the purpose.

2. Believe it

The difference between aiming for a specific outcome versus just *hoping* for a good outcome comes down to the beliefs you have and how you feel about what you have written in your outcome statement.

When you read your outcome statement to yourself what thoughts/beliefs do you have? Remember to make a note of them. Does your statement state one thing and your thoughts say the opposite? Are your thoughts saying, *How are you going to achieve that?* Can you see your outcome statement being a reality in the future? When you read it do you feel good and can you imagine it being your reality?

Your objective here is to *believe* the scenario and to *feel good* and inspired when you read it. This is where recognising your thoughts and beliefs is crucial to understanding whether the outcome you have written is an intention or just a hope. Read it as many times as you need to, until it sounds believable to you. Tweak it a few times to find the words that sound right to you. It's yours: you can change it until it feels right. Try not to dumb down your outcome statement to make it feel right. If you can identify the belief that's making it seem impossible, remove the belief rather than change the statement.

3. Read it and visualise it

When you have the final version, continue reading it, aloud if possible, a couple of times a day. Do this when you first

O = Outcome

arrive at your desk to begin your day and at the end of your day before you leave your office. When you wake up in the morning and get into bed in the evening are also ideal times.

In addition to reading the statement, *visualise* it. Imagine yourself already there, how you feel, who is with you, how you are dressed, the building you are in, the people around you. The more detail you can picture, the more real it will appear, which makes it more achievable to visualise and feel. You may even want to collect some images to represent your vision and create a vision board.

The more familiar the statement and its content become, the more your mind will set in motion a way of achieving what you are stating and *seeing*. You will start to have ideas, you will meet people who can help, opportunities will show up that are directly related to the changes you want to make. This is exactly how we feed our Reticular Activating System (RAS), detailed in Chapter 3.

4. Action

As these inspired ideas and opportunities come to you, list them, follow them up, and begin to take action. At times, the action may be a tiny step that isn't going to change anything drastically. That's OK – lots of small steps still create movement in the right direction.

I cannot tell you how long any of this will take to happen, however I can tell you it works. Your contribution to the process is to *believe* your statement and to follow up any thoughts, ideas and opportunities that show up. It's ideal if you can continue to work on your business as usual and have your outcome statement as a side project rather than focusing on it so much that you get frustrated with the pace at which it's happening.

The one thing I want to stress here is that action does not mean you going all out to make your outcome statement become a reality. When you have a clear idea of what you hope will happen, the universe has an impressive way of magically sending you an inspired idea, and what and whom you need – it is *then* that you take action. An inspired idea from the universe usually appears in the form of a gut feeling, or you wake up with a totally random idea, so listen to your gut and follow your instincts.

5. Future decisions

Your outcome statement represents where you are heading. In order to stay on track, ensure that all future decisions are in line with your vision and are *not* going to take you totally off-course. Sometimes it's hard to say no to a new client or some additional income, but if it is going to take you in a totally different direction with no synergy to where you are

O = Outcome

heading, or if it's going to distract you from your plans, think twice before accepting it.

This five-step formula can be used with any situation you wish to change. You may find it useful and want to try it for a personal scenario, too.

Here's an example from Josh:
Josh loves servicing his clients. He has a boutique graphic design business, which began three years ago. He is a talented designer and he's always exceeding his clients' expectations. Josh's current situation is that he really dreads having to constantly find new clients, even though without them he wouldn't have a business.

Josh's current attempt at finding new clients:
Currently, Josh does a lot of hoping and wishing for his clients. He knows that he needs to constantly find new business but when it comes to it he uses any excuse not to and then when his current client's work is complete he has no clients and has to find more.

Josh has social media accounts, a website and a well-designed postcard/flyer. Marketing materials and platforms are necessary for Josh, but they're not enough to secure a client. Josh knows that securing a client almost always requires some personal contact with them. This is the part he dreads. He's scared they will think his prices are too high. He's worried they may not like his style of work. He thinks he will be judged because he has tattoos. He doesn't feel confident talking to someone from a non-creative industry (which is where most of his clients are from). All of these beliefs compound each time he has to find new clients.

Josh's outcome statement:

It's been two months now since I started to attract new clients. I now have the confidence to talk about my business to potential clients both face-to-face and on the phone because I believe in what I do. My previous clients are recommending me to their clients and colleagues. I attend two networking meetings each month and I am regularly asked to do a presentation on the basics of design – this always brings in a couple more clients.

I am so busy now that I have a personal assistant who finds new networking opportunities for me and puts my name forward for talks. I really enjoy attracting new clients to my business and I have built some amazing relationships in the process.

What Josh discovered when he read his statement:

Once Josh had his final statement, which took a couple of attempts, he read it a few times until he was comfortable with it. Each time he read it he could begin to see what needed to be done to make it become a reality. He realised immediately that the doubt he had about his prices, his style of work, and his image had never been a problem with any of his clients in the past. In fact, his clients love his style of work and his image. He was assuming (believing) they wouldn't because they're not creative people themselves.

O = Outcome

Josh's actions:
1. Say yes to speaking opportunities. I love talking about design and if people can see my passion and understanding they are more likely to use my services.
2. Book into a networking meeting – just do it! Until I know what it's like, I'm filling myself with doubt and fear!
3. Remove the belief that potential clients will question my pricing.
4. Remove the belief that potential clients will not like my style of work.
5. Remove the belief that potential clients will judge me because I have tattoos.
6. 6. Own my image. I am a creative and this is how I choose to look. If a person is not comfortable with my image, they are not my client.

Josh's future decisions

Prior to creating my outcome statement I would turn down many invitations, perceiving them as a waste of my time. Now when I am invited to an event by a friend, colleague, client or supplier if I am available I accept because I can see the potential opportunity that could be at that event. My new philosophy is the more people I meet the more chance I have of them becoming clients at some point.

Josh's example should help with the stages of your own outcome statement.

Exercise 2
Setting Intentions

This exercise could work as a continuation of Exercise 1 or you may wish to look at a totally different area of your business for this exercise.

Intention is another word for goal. I use the word intention as I feel it is more personal and I feel like I am making more of a commitment to myself. Regardless of what you choose to call it the concept is to create some steps or a to-do list towards the outcome you desire.

Here are my seven steps for setting an intention.

Step 1:
Write it down

Studies have shown that goals (intentions) that are written down have a 42% greater chance of being achieved than those that remain in your mind (Morrissey, 2017).

O = Outcome

Step 2:
Write it in the present tense as though it has already come to fruition

The subconscious mind constantly receives instructions from you through your thoughts. It does not have the ability to decipher whether the thought is something you want or not, real or not, beneficial to you or not – it just carries out what your thoughts are telling it.

Writing the intention in the present tense sends a different message than the future or past tense and this contributes to how your mind processes it.

Past tense: I used to have the car of my dreams, now I'd love another.

Future tense: I will have the car of my dreams.

Present tense: I have the car of my dreams and it feels fantastic.

If you tell yourself you used to have something, your subconscious mind will keep reminding you that you used to have it and you don't now.

If you tell yourself you will have something, your subconscious mind will keep you in the suspense of waiting and waiting for that one day – which we all know is not a day of the week.

If you tell yourself you have something, your subconscious mind will respond as though you have it and that will open opportunities to make it happen.

Step 3:
Believe what you are writing

The most important part of an intention is that you can believe it's possible. You don't need to know how or exactly when, but you do need to believe it is possible.

In Chapter 3, I outlined what a belief is – it's a thought that you continually think until it becomes real or true to you. So, if you have written, I have the car of my dreams and it feels fantastic, but a thought is saying, Uh, no you don't, you drive your dad's old car, or, It's just that, buddy, a car of your dreams: it's not real, what those thoughts do is immediately counteract the intention. Those thoughts are your lemon juice, what you *really* believe.

> *Know your lemon juice: If this happens, write down the thoughts. You can remove them using a process in Chapter 10.*

Believing a new intention can take time. Keep saying it to yourself, visualising it and imagining the feeling of having achieved it. At some point, and it could take an hour or a week, you will say it and feel yourself actually believing it. That's the feeling you are aiming for with all your intentions.

O = Outcome

If you write them without the corresponding feeling the doubts will creep in and keep you where you are.

Step 4:
Using numbers (dates, values, amounts) when setting an intention

Using numbers can motivate but equally they can restrict.

How using numbers can be restricting

Most intention setting rules include using numbers – a date or a specific amount. Here's why I see this as restricting. If I set the intention, I will have $100,000 in my bank account by 30 June this year, it creates two things. Firstly, it restricts the amount to $100,000, which at the time of setting the intention was substantially more than I currently had, but why put a limit on it? If I can attract more, I would love to. Also, if only $91,500 is in my bank account by that date, it will register as a fail in my subconscious. Secondly, the date creates a deadline for when the money needs to appear creating an identifiable fail if the money is not in my bank account by then.

An alternative way to write the same intention could be: I always have more than enough money in my bank account to fund my chosen lifestyle. Or, if it's money for a particular purchase: I have enough money to purchase the car of my dreams when the time is right. The reason I suggest when the time is right is because we've all been in a position where we want something to happen at a certain time and it doesn't. When it eventually does happen we can see how the timing was perfect and that any sooner would not have been the right time.

Please be aware that this is only a suggestion – using numbers does create outcomes. I see the energy attached to a number-related intention impacting it manifesting or not. For example, if the intention is for a set amount of money by a set date because I need the money to pay for X which is urgent, I could potentially create a set of conditions around the intention and surround it with urgency, worry and desperation, leading to me thinking about it 24/7. In my experience this distorts the manifesting. If the energy attached to the number-related intention is that of not being dependent on it happening, so the intention is all but forgotten, the opposite can happen. See below.

Using figures can work

Here's a personal example of how figures do work. I was recently asked by my coach to set a financial goal for the following six weeks. I was experiencing such a financial challenge at the time that I wrote: I have $10k in my bank account by [date]. My energy towards that goal was one of: I've got nothing to lose and that would be great and then I totally forgot about it.

O = Outcome

Five weeks later, with my financial situation still challenging me, I was gifted $7,000. It came from somebody who knew what I was going through, but I had not asked them for any money. When I looked at my bank account over the past six weeks what I saw blew me away. There was a deposit of $2000 (a friend had lent me money to pay my rent) and $1000 (a loan from another friend), plus the $7000 gifted. There in my bank account was a total of $10k that I had received in that six-week period. In my opinion, me letting go* of the outcome actually made it happen.

*My definition of the term letting go is to not be attached to the outcome. If the money appears – fantastic. If the money doesn't appear, that's OK, too. Letting go can often be the hardest part of setting intentions.

Step 5:
Let it be

Finally, once you are happy with your intention, let it be. Don't question it, don't doubt it, don't try to force it to happen – just let it be.

Compare your intention with planting a seed, literally. Once a seed is planted in the soil we leave it, we water it and wait. We don't go back and dig it up and check it's still there, because we know it's still there. We don't get frustrated with it because it's taking so long to grow. We don't plant another seed in the hope that one grows quicker. Let your intention happen in its own time. Yes, you may have to take some action (watering it), but it will appear at the perfect time.

Step 6:
Pushing or pulling?

Being aware of whether your intention is pushing you away or pulling you towards something can also impact the outcome of your intention.

Here's a simple example:

Present tense intention: I am financially rich.

Why would someone set this intention? It could be pushing them away from having been or currently being poor. Or it could be pulling them towards the desire to have things they've never had before. Every intention has a push or pull (belief) behind it.

Every intention also has a feeling you are hoping to experience once the intention has manifested. Know what feeling you hope to have when your intention has manifested and begin to feel it now. I saw a quote recently that said, 'Beware of destination addiction – a preoccupation with the idea that happiness is in the next place, the next job or with the next partner. Until you give up the idea that happiness

O = Outcome

is somewhere else, it will never be where you are'. The word happiness in this quote can be replaced with whatever feeling you are wanting and waiting to experience.

Here's a secret: the push or pull of an intention and the hope of experiencing a feeling once your intention has manifested are both conditions placed on that intention and will interfere with its manifestation. Once you are aware of the reasons behind your intention let them go.

If you have an attachment to the outcome of an intention, it will be harder for it to be achieved because you have expectations on it and you will be looking for those expectations rather than letting the process unfold in its own way. Potentially, you will not be satisfied with any amount of money because it is unlikely you could ever feel rich if your focus is not feeling poor. Yes, the bank account could have three million dollars in it, but you could still feel poor – because that is a familiar feeling. Being rich is an unknown feeling, so you will never know when you have achieved it.

Alternatively, there's a chance you could get caught in the cycle of always needing to have more, even after you have acquired your list of things, because you still don't feel rich. Knowing your push or pull and then detaching from it enables you to appreciate your current situation – which is always your life now, in this present moment. The beliefs creating your push or pull can be removed.

Step 7:
Be grateful

The concept of gratitude – being grateful for something – is either a practice you have formed or you *intend* to get around to. It's one of those all or nothing areas. If you already consciously appreciate the things you are grateful for in your life, keep it up. If you *intend* to start being grateful, now is the time.

Gratitude is a simple concept of acknowledging all the things in your life that you appreciate. In order for you to remember to do this, creating your own practice is recommended. For example, you may choose to write down three things you are grateful for before you go to sleep each night, or you may include those things in your prayers. Some families share their lists around the dinner table. This is a great way to introduce the concept to children. If you drive or commute to work, you may choose to focus on gratitude then. There's no set formula that works better, it's about finding what works best for you.

Being grateful for what you currently have, regardless of what that is, will create a positive feeling in you.

You can be grateful for catching the flu. Why?

O = Outcome

Because it enables you to rest – something you don't allow yourself to do. You can be grateful for the car you drive, even if it is not your *ideal* car. Why? Because it gives you the ability to travel easily to where you need to be.

Even if life is only a fraction better than yesterday, you're moving in the right direction and that's something to be grateful for.

Another way of being grateful is to consciously say *thank you* for the mundane things that happen during the day. We've become a society driven by *achieving* and *having*, to create a persona say thank you for the little things – having an umbrella when it rains, the busker with the great voice who makes you smile, someone holding a door for you, even the guy filling the shelves in the supermarket. Our day would be very different without these *little* things.

> *Know your lemon juice: Don't forget to jot down any thoughts you have during this exercise.*

Exercise 3
Visual Journal

This exercise is one I love to deliver in my Believe workshops. I have yet to find anyone who hasn't enjoyed it – even the guys.

Being creative is innate in everyone, according to Stuart Brown, who began life as a violence researcher in the US, but became a play researcher after analysing data about the boy who carried out the first mass school shooting at the University of Texas in 1966. What Brown discovered from a number of different specialists who investigated the boy's life was that Charles Whitman, who the previous evening stabbed his wife and mother to death at their individual homes, had been raised by a very strict father and was not allowed to play (be creative, use his imagination) and consequently that lack of creative expression had built up and turned into violence. In his Ted Talk on play, Stuart Brown claims the opposite of play is not work; it's depression, which frequently builds up into violence. Stuart Brown has also written a book – details of both can be found in the additional reading section at the end of this book.

The pressure and expectation we currently put on ourselves to achieve is beyond ridiculous. The more *things* we *have to*

O = Outcome

do, the less time we have to relax, reflect or just stop. We no longer have an official day of rest. It wasn't that long ago that a Sunday was a day when the shops were closed and the churches were open. This pace is unsustainable, so before you hit the wall and are forced to stop, learn to build into your week (or month, at least) a time to play or be creative.

Creativity is natural. Watch children play together – their imaginations can create all sorts of scenarios from just a cardboard box. They can play for hours with a doll or a couple of cars, they don't need instructions or direction, and their free-flowing ideas play out beautifully. As we get older and start high school, opportunities to be creative become less and less until eventually we opt out of art because it's not perceived as a serious subject.

This is your opportunity to revisit your creativity.

> *Know your lemon juice: At this point you may be considering skipping the next couple of pages for fear of having to draw something. Don't forget to write down any feelings or thoughts, even memories that come to mind from your school days.*

Researcher Brene Brown has studied hundreds of thousands of people over the years. One interesting discovery she made was that around 85% of the people she spoke with were shamed at school by a teacher, which prevented them from ever taking up further learning. Of that 85% over 50% had what Brown has termed *art scars* – a shaming of their creative work at school, leaving them convinced they are creatively talentless (*Brene Brown on Creativity*, 2015). This is how I felt when my art teacher told me I couldn't draw. Not surprisingly, I have seen people shrink in my workshops when they learn they're about to be creative.

This doesn't require too much talent, just your imagination.

What you need:

1. A pre-loved hardback book – you can pick one up for $1 at an op shop.
2. Some magazines – again, often available for .20c at an op shop.
3. A pair of scissors.
4. A glue stick.

This is a mix of journaling and mini vision boarding.

Firstly, if the book is old the paper pages may be very thin. If they are, stick a couple of pages together to strengthen your canvas.

The objective is to express your thoughts and desires through cutting and pasting pictures from the magazines.

O = Outcome

What you create does not have to be a masterpiece or business related. Being creative is another tool to discover something about yourself and help you switch off when you need to.

Where to begin? It's your choice!

Here are some ideas to get you started:

- You could put your dreams in your journal.

- You could create a mini vision board for your business or to match your outcome statement.

- You could choose a colour and cut out as many things as you can find in that colour.

- You could design your ideal home.

- You could stick in pictures of the type of people you want to attract as clients.

- You could cut out words.

- You could draw or doodle.

Your options are only limited by you.

The idea of using a book keeps the activity compact. You don't need to clear the dining table and make a mess. This is an activity that can be done on your knees, sitting in the lounge room. If you have kids, this is an easy activity for them to do also. The important thing is it is enabling you to use your imagination. Nobody needs to see what you have done; it's not about being an artist. If you can make visual journaling a weekly habit, you will begin to feel different.

Post-exercise suggestion: *On completion of the exercises you will have a list of beliefs, thoughts, feelings and actions around this particular topic that you are now consciously aware of. Your objective is to discover the underlying belief(s). If you are not sure what the belief is, you can go back to the section called Exploring Your Own Thoughts in Chapter 3 to explore the thought some more. Once you have a list of beliefs, you can choose to manage, change or remove them. How to do this is outlined in Chapter 10.*

'Don't stay in bed, unless you can make money in bed.'

George Burns, American comedian, actor, singer
and writer, 1896 – 1996.

W
= Wealth

Chapter 7
For What it's Worth

I started Chapter 5 by suggesting if you only read one chapter make it that one. Well, you need to read at least two chapters – this is the other.

Wealth: *an abundance or profusion of anything.*

I love the definition of wealth. Without it the word wealth to most people conjures up thoughts of money. Wealth is an abundance of *anything*, which makes us all wealthy.

There are two very different components to wealth – *being* wealthy (having stuff) and *feeling* wealthy (possible whether you have stuff or not).

I know people who have accumulated lots of stuff – big house, cars, motorbike, beautiful clothes – which could be perceived as *being* wealthy, but I know they don't *feel* wealthy. They continue to strive for more, trying to create the feeling of wealth even though they don't actually know what *wealthy* feels like. (You may want to refer back to Chapter 6 and re-read step six of exercise two.)

The purpose of this chapter is to explore your overall view of wealth and for you to specifically find your own perception of wealth relating to your business, *including* money.

Your wealth is a reflection of your own self-worth and your self-worth only attracts what you *believe* you are worth, so take a look around you. What's happening in relation to wealth in your business? What type of clients are you attracting? How much income are you generating? Are you spending your income as quickly as you are receiving it? Be aware of how wealthy you *feel*. Would you like more stuff? The exercises in this chapter will help you see, through your current beliefs, why your business is like it is and why your life is as it is.

If a person (unknowingly) doesn't deem him/herself worthy of obtaining or having something, they could find it exceptionally difficult to achieve it. This is a great place for you to start recognising your own beliefs around

W = Wealth

worth. What eludes you? What is appearing unattainable? What did you have that you lost? You probably have an explanation as to why, but underneath that reason is a core belief connected to you not being *worthy* of having it.

An obvious and repeated example of this is everyday people winning the lottery and becoming very wealthy overnight, only to end up broke or in debt a relatively short time later. Spending the money from a lottery win in a short period of time could be perceived as the person enjoying life – having an expensive holiday, paying off their debts, helping out friends and family members or upgrading their home/car/wardrobe. This could also be perceived as wanting to get rid of the money quickly because subconsciously they don't feel they are worthy of having such a *huge* amount, comparative to what they are comfortable with.

> *Know your lemon juice: Remember to make a note of any statements or thoughts that pop into your head while focusing on this topic. You can do this in your BIYB workbook or on a sheet of paper.*

Your self-worth can be measured in different ways. By the type of friends you have: are they caring, compassionate supporters of you or do they constantly take from you? Your work environment: is it a clean and tidy place that you love to walk into or is it just somewhere to base yourself for now? The work you do: does it give you satisfaction and inspire you, or is it soul destroying? The way you present yourself: do you take pride in your appearance or do you stay in your PJs at every opportunity? Your health: do you take care of your body by exercising and eating well, or do you abuse your body with alcohol, cigarettes, drugs and sugar? All of these areas are reflecting the worth *you* hold for *you*.

The aim is to find a balance across all areas of your life by recognising the beliefs that have distorted your perception of what you believe you deserve. There are some famous people who are extremely wealthy and live grandiose lifestyles who are morbidly obese, or fighting an addiction, or living with a debilitating disease – that's an example of unbalanced self-worth. Even though it appears to be only showing up in a person's health, it will be impacting other areas of their life, directly or indirectly. Knowing the underlying cause creates the choice to change or remove that belief, producing a knock-on effect to allow more wealth in.

When it comes to money, talking about it doesn't come naturally or easily to many people and can stir a range of different emotions from defensiveness to indifference.

You subconsciously learn your financial worth at an early age, as you pick up information from the world around you – for example, the conversations you hear between your parents or the comments about how much things cost. As

W = Wealth

mentioned earlier, I grew up in a working class family in the North of England. Both my parents worked hard to provide for us four children and I never felt that we missed out. We always had a Santa sack full of presents at Christmas and birthday parties.

We also went on annual caravanning holidays and as much as we enjoyed them we were aware it was too expensive to go overseas. This environment, along with hearing the expressions, 'Money doesn't grow on trees,' and, 'That's how the other half live,' was *normal* when I was growing up and the statements appeared true for us at the time – I'm not denying that. However, what this information did was potentially set me up to continue living this way, because that became my normal, which created a money comfort zone where it was much easier to stay because it was familiar.

Although these money beliefs appear to be real, they aren't. They are *one* perspective of money and a lifestyle and can be changed.

However you were raised, whatever your perception of money when growing up, you can break that pattern. There are many stories of people born into unimaginable poverty and homelessness becoming multi-millionaires. Fashion designer Ralph Lauren, now worth $5.9 billion according to Forbes, says, 'When I'd get my brother's hand-me-downs, there was an energy in me that made me say, 'I want to get my own things, to make my own statement'. Somewhere along the line, that energy — coupled with my exposure, through movies, to a world I hadn't known — turned into something.'

TV show host Oprah Winfrey, now worth $3.1 billion according to Forbes, says, 'The whole idea, I think, of having wealth is not letting wealth use you but you use it. Being a person who has come from an outhouse, and very poor circumstances, I can assure you that the more money you get, it really doesn't change you — unless you are the kind of person who is defined by money'.

Howard Schultz, Chairman and CEO of Starbucks, now worth $2.9 billion according to Forbes, said, 'When I was seven years old, I experienced something that deeply affected me that I carry with me every single day, and that is the scar and the shame of being a poor kid living in government-subsidised housing'.

The way you live your life is *your* choice. The easy way is the way you have always known, the way you were taught to live and there is nothing wrong with that if you are happy with your life. But if you are wandering around wishing things were different – they can be. You've heard the famous saying from Albert Einstein, 'The definition of insanity is doing the same thing over and over again, but expecting different results'.

W = Wealth

Well, that sums up perfectly what not to do if you want something to change. As embedded as some beliefs are it is possible to change all of them.

The exercises in this chapter may prove to be the most challenging in this book.

Pre-exercise suggestion: *Prior to beginning any of the exercises, use the BIYB Workbook which you can download from www.believeinyourbusiness. info or, if you don't have the workbook, have a piece of paper or notebook available to answer the questions and catch those first, fleeting, thoughts and beliefs. You may perceive them as reasons you don't have to do a specific exercise (aka excuses). If that's how they come to you, still jot them down. You could possibly get a feeling like dread or anxiety or even elation or excitement, or you may find yourself physically avoiding the exercise by leaving the room to get another drink. This, too, is vital information, so write it down. The more you can capture what is going on in your mind and body when confronted with particular tasks, the more lemon juice you will discover.*

With the following set of exercises you will gain the most benefit if you are able to *feel* your body's responses and follow them rather than complete the answers logically. I have delivered these exercises many times in workshops and without any exception it is the one topic that generates the most heated debates. Money definitely challenges people's beliefs and stirs emotions. Listen to your thoughts carefully and feel what your body is telling you.

Exercise 1
Word association

With this exercise what comes out of your mouth is important, however, what you are *feeling* and *thinking* when you speak is equally as valuable to you.

Word association can be played with a partner or alone. In both cases you will require a table to fill out, like the one shown below. If you have downloaded the BIYB workbook you will find a blank table in there, plus a list of words. If you are playing with a partner give them the list of words (also listed in the diagram) for them to read out to you.

If you are doing the exercise alone, cut out the eighteen words from the workbook or if you don't have the workbook cut up a piece of paper into eighteen pieces and write a word on each one. Turn the papers face down and randomly choose one at a time. This way you will be able to catch your feelings more easily than reading the words from the list, seeing the next word and pre-empting a response.

The concept of word association is to say the *first* thing that comes to you when you see the word you are playing with. Write down what you said and then consider what you were *thinking* or *feeling*, at the same time. The quicker you play it, the more telling your responses can be.

W = Wealth

As you work through this exercise you may say some words and trigger some feelings you weren't expecting. You may also stall with some words – avoid analysing them too much. Just write them down until you have completed all eighteen.

	What you said	What you felt/thought
Twenty dollars		
Government subsidy		
Friends		
Worth		
Struggle		
Business		
Money		
Homeless		
Happy		
Luxury		
Lack		
Value		
Bank account		
Sick		
Enough		
Possessions		
Greed		
Abundance		

Know your lemon juice

Hopefully you have a list of juicy feelings and thoughts that unexpectedly popped up during that exercise. When I have delivered this exercise with mentoring clients there are usually one or two words from the list that stand out to me as unusual or limiting responses. I would just focus on those two words and dig a bit deeper. Sometimes clients are surprised at their own responses or feelings and so we focus on those words, too.

Read through the list again, including your response word and corresponding feelings/thoughts, and see which one(s) stands out for you. You don't have to explore all your answers but there will be a couple that are showing you a disconnect between what you said and what you thought. Can you find the underlying belief? You can always re-read Chapter 3: Recognising Your Beliefs to assist with finding what the underlying belief is.

Exercise 2

What would you do with an endless flow of money?

This is (for most of us) a hypothetical scenario. If you had an endless flow of money coming in, as much as you choose, every day, without you having to do anything except receive it, what would you do with it?

W = Wealth

How does it make you feel? What's different for you? Does your business still exist in your new financial world? There is no right or wrong answer to this question; however, knowing *why* you want money will help to attract it.

You can either use the space in the BIYB workbook or just use a piece of paper. Write down what you would do, how you would live, and where you would live. Would you travel? Would you do the things on your One Day list? This exercise may benefit from a first draft then a revisit a couple of days later. This is something few people have even thought about so it can feel quite daunting. If you feel that way, tell yourself it's just pretend and your logical thoughts will take a backseat because it's nothing to worry about, it's just pretend!

I have been asked by clients when doing this exercise, 'Can I put X, Y, or Z?' or, 'Is it too greedy to ask for X, Y or Z?' These examples are highlighting their beliefs. If *you* need permission to do this, this is your permission. You can write whatever you want.

> *Know your lemon juice: This is a great time to catch your thoughts.*

Exercise 3
Giving

1. Money can buy happiness.

Studies by Robert H Frank, author of *Luxury Fever: Why Money Fails to Satisfy in an Era of Excess*, show that the positive feelings we get from buying material objects (known to some as retail therapy) are frustratingly fleeting. Spending money on experiences, especially ones with other people, produces positive emotions that are both meaningful and more lasting.

In an article for inc.com titled *Money Can Really Buy Happiness if You Spend it These 4 Ways, According to Science*, Minda Zetlin wrote: 'When researchers gave college students some extra cash and instructed one group to spend it on themselves and another group to spend it on others, the second group reported much more happiness than the first.

'It makes sense if you think about our social orientation – giving money away or spending it on someone else makes us feel more connected to others. (As well as proud of our own generosity.) The thanks and warm fuzzies we get from the recipient of our largesse is likely to make us feel good as well. So go ahead and buy that nice present or make that charitable donation. You'll be making yourself happier, as well as others.'

2. Giving is good for your health

A wide range of research has linked different forms of generosity to better health, even among the sick and elderly. In his co-written book with Jill Neimark, *Why Good Things Happen to Good* People, Stephen Post, a professor of preventative medicine at Stony Brook University, reports that giving to others has been shown to increase health benefits in people with chronic illness, including HIV and multiple sclerosis. Research suggests that one reason giving may improve physical health and longevity is that it helps decrease stress, which is associated with a variety of health problems.

3. Giving promotes cooperation and social connection

When you give you're more likely to get back. Several studies, including work by sociologists Brent Simpson and Robb Willer, have suggested that when you give to others, your generosity is likely to be rewarded by others down the line – sometimes by the person you gave to, sometimes by someone else. As researcher John Cacioppo writes in his book *Loneliness: Human Nature and the Need for Social Connection*, 'The more extensive the reciprocal altruism born of social connection [...] the greater the advance toward health, wealth, and happiness'.

4. Giving evokes gratitude

Whether you're on the giving or receiving end of a gift, that gift can elicit feelings of gratitude – it can be a way of expressing gratitude or instilling gratitude in the recipient. And research has found that gratitude is integral to happiness, health, and social bonds. Robert Emmons and Michael McCullough, co-directors of the Research Project on Gratitude and Thankfulness, found that teaching college students to count their blessings and cultivate gratitude caused them to exercise more, be more optimistic, and feel better about their lives overall.

5. Giving is contagious

When you give you don't only help the immediate recipient of your gift. You also spur a ripple effect of generosity through your community.

Your giving consciously exercise

Over the next few weeks, become conscious of the giving and receiving you do. Make two lists at the end of each day. One of things you gave – a helping hand, a compliment or your time. The second of the things you received – a coffee, a kiss, or a compliment. This is not a competition or a reason to complain that you give more than you receive, it is for you to see the difference in how you feel when you give and receive and watch as they increase.

W = Wealth

The more you give, the more you will receive and the more you receive, the more you have to be grateful for.

Post-exercise suggestion: *On completion of the exercises you will have a list of beliefs, thoughts, feelings and actions around this particular topic that you are now consciously aware of. Your objective is to discover the underlying belief(s). If you are not sure what the belief is, you can go back to the section called Exploring Your Own Thoughts in Chapter 3 to explore the thought some more. Once you have a list of beliefs, you can choose to manage, change or remove them. How to do this is outlined in Chapter 10.*

'As soon as you trust yourself, you will know how to live.'

Johann Wolfgang von Goethe, poet, novelist, playwright (*Faust*) **and statesman, 1749 – 1832.**

T
= Trust

Chapter 8

Is it Luck?

Do you know somebody that you refer to as lucky because things always seem to work out for them, whether it's their home life or their business?

What is luck and who is Lady Luck? Luck is described as success or failure apparently brought on by chance rather than through one's own actions. And Lady Luck is the mythical woman we can thank or blame depending on the outcome.

Superstition is another source we perceive as having the ability to bring us success or failure. My mum knows and has lived by many superstitions: it's bad luck to walk under a ladder; a black cat walking across your path will bring you good luck; an itchy nose means you're going to have a fight; cross knives and you'll be kissed, crossed or cursed; a knife on the floor means a man at the door; it's unlucky to change your clothes if you put them on inside out. I could actually go on and on, more were coming to mind as I was writing. I grew up listening to these superstitions and believed them until one day in my late teens I realised I couldn't let some old wives' tales dictate my life, plus there were so many I was constantly second-guessing. However, my best friend Mandy (actually Amanda J Ward, a name I always thought sounded famous at school), who also heard many of these superstitions from my mum took on all of them and to this day still thinks of my mum whenever something superstitious happens. This is a great example of, 'If you believe you can or you believe you can't, you're right,' made famous by Henry Ford. It literally comes down to choice.

Does luck and/or superstition give you something to blame if things don't go the way you'd hoped and give you something to credit when things do work out? Are they creating something to hide behind so the outcome is one step removed from you and you don't have to trust or believe in yourself?

Your experiences around trust up to this point are likely to revolve around external factors: a person who you trusted that let you down or a concept or product you had faith in

T = Trust

not performing to your expectations. In this chapter you are going to focus on the trust you have in *yourself*. Blame is a very convenient shield that all of us have tried to hide behind at some point in our lives only to discover that deep down we made a *choice* to be part of the situation – the relationship, the major purchase, or the client pitch.

When it comes to running a business or managing a business team, trust is omnipresent. The fact that you are in this position shows you have a degree of faith in yourself and if you reflect on some of the things you have achieved to this point you will see you do trust yourself. Becoming conscious of the belief you have in yourself gives you the opportunity to test that belief more and gives you the confidence to step further outside of your comfort zone and grow.

Trusting yourself has many facets. If you have your driving licence, you can get in a car and drive and you trust yourself to drive. If you are going hiking and you have a map you will trust your ability to read the map and reach the destination. What if there is no guidance or evidence for an outcome when making a decision? That is frequently the case when running a business. How do you decide what to do? How many times have you known what to do but ignored that feeling and made a different, more practical or logical decision? I'm guessing a few.

Having belief in and trusting *yourself* as a business owner is arguably your greatest asset. Even when you have a team of advisors or a respected mentor who you can discuss information with, ultimately *you* need to make the final decision. Others will have a different perspective than you. Their views are valuable as it broadens your awareness, however, ultimately it's your decision. This is where your instinct or your gut feeling can be your most trusted source.

You can choose to avoid or ignore this concept and still run a successful business, however it could prove to be a rocky road. I have faith that you as a reader of this book will already have a degree of trust in yourself that you will benefit from strengthening.

The following exercises will enable you to gauge where you currently stand on trust and how healthy your self-belief is.

Pre-exercise suggestion: *Prior to beginning any of the exercises, use the BIYB Workbook which you can download from www.believeinyourbusiness. info or, if you don't have the workbook, have a piece of paper or notebook available to answer the questions and catch those first, fleeting thoughts and beliefs. You may perceive them as reasons you don't have to do a specific exercise (aka excuses). If that's how they come to you, still jot them down. You could possibly get a feeling like dread or anxiety or even elation or excitement; or you may find yourself physically avoiding the exercise by leaving the room to get another drink. This, too, is vital information, so write it down. The more you can capture of what is going on in your mind and body when confronted with particular tasks, the more lemon juice you will discover.*

T = Trust

Exercise 1
Trusting in and receiving from a power greater than us

We've all experienced a coincidence. A *common* coincidence is when you think about a person that you haven't seen for a while (let's call them Bob), and the following day you see Bob in the street or Bob calls you. Sometimes these coincidences will blow your mind and other times they go unnoticed, however, they are happening to us all the time.

The process of the above coincidence works like this:

1. Something causes you to have a thought about Bob (you see a picture of a guy who reminds you of Bob from school and you think, I wonder how Bob is). This could be a fleeting thought or could be more deliberate.
2. You let the thought go, meaning you don't sit and dwell on it.
3. Your Reticular Activating System hears your thought (however fleeting) and sends a vibration out to find out how Bob is and bring your path and Bob's path together.
4. The following day you bump into Bob in the street. (Now you can ask him how he is.)

Here is where your beliefs kick in. Do you believe seeing Bob was a pure coincidence, a one-off? Or do you believe that your thought about Bob set the wheels in motion for the universe to arrange for the two of you to cross paths?

Imagine if your thought created the whole process and that *all* your thoughts were delivered to you. This doesn't sound possible when you first hear it because it is not common science and is definitely not what you were taught in school. Quantum mechanics, however, can now prove that all our thoughts send out vibrations to find or attract a matching vibration (Emmons & McCullough, n.d.). The power greater than us uses the emotion around the thought to draw the matching vibrations together and your RAS picks up what you are asking for. This is why what we call a bad day or a good day usually lasts the whole day. As soon as the first thing goes wrong on a bad day we subconsciously send out the thought, *What else could go wrong today?* Your RAS obeys your instruction and finds more things to go wrong throughout the day. The same applies to a good day, when everything seems to go right. If you change your thoughts during the day, you will change your day.

What you choose to call a power greater than us is also your choice. You may call it God or Buddha, the universe, guidance, spirit, source – it really doesn't matter what you call it but it will be a huge advantage if you believe it and trust it. I choose to call it the universe.

T = Trust

When we think of something we *really* want or need to happen we can become impatient and try to *make* it happen ourselves. During this process we can feel desperate and frustrated. As the emotion around the thought or request is key to the vibration being sent out, this will lead to us drawing more things that cause us to feel desperate and frustrated. Here's an example: if you want a new customer or client *because* you're not reaching target this month, the thought is likely to be shrouded with lack and fear. The vibrations of lack and fear will be the prominent emotions being sent out and that's what will be attracted. In this case, the concept of simply trusting a power greater than us feels impossible. Discovering why you feel lack and fear is something you can do, then find the belief, remove it and send the same thought out to the universe.

I've introduced this concept here as a new way to approach decision-making. For those who are aware of this it's purely a reminder. The universe is constantly available to us. It is our choice to consciously ask it and trust it.

Please note: The ability to manifest and be guided is a learned process. I am not suggesting you throw a list of requests to the universe and go on holiday expecting to return and find everything has come to fruition and is ticking along nicely. I am suggesting, however, the more aware you become of the underlying thoughts you have around decisions you make the more you will see how occasionally you get in your own way and end up on the rocky road.

I have listed in the additional reading section at the back of this book some books and talks available that relate to manifesting and universal guidance.

Equally important for this concept to work is the ability to be able to receive. As strange as this sounds I have personally experienced consciously being in receiving mode and it's different from just assuming I'm in receiving mode. Referring back to the example of having a bad day: it's highly unlikely that even one amazingly good thing is going to happen because on a bad day our RAS is not looking for amazingly good things, only more bad stuff to keep the bad day bad. Therefore you can only receive things that match your mood. Strictly speaking, you are always able to receive, but you are not always going to receive what you expect.

The way to tell what you are open to receiving is to observe what you have recently received. It could be a compliment, a pay rise, a cup of coffee, or it could be a parking fine, an argument or someone stealing your wallet. Only you will know what you are open to receiving. If it's been a while since you received something good this exercise hopefully will change that.

T = Trust

This exercise gives you the opportunity to see how the universe responds to your requests, thoughts and emotions.

Begin by asking the universe to send you something that you consider easy so you can check two things. Firstly, that the universe does hear you and is on your side and secondly, that you are in receiving mode.

Making what you ask for easy and not life-changing (although it could turn out to be) will remove any emotion from it, enabling it to flow more freely to you – just like how Bob appeared when you didn't really care if he did or not.

> *Know your lemon juice: This may have caused you to question a few things, which is a good sign. Please write your thoughts down so you can explore them more.*

Write down each step as you do it. There is space in your BIYB workbook for this exercise.

1. Create a time frame, so that you are not waiting forever.
- Anything from a few hours to three days.
2. Ask for something general but not too specific.
- To experience something that makes you laugh out loud, or makes you smile, or takes your breath away.
- To be given a tangible gift (remember not all gifts come gift wrapped!).

- To meet an interesting person.
- To receive a compliment.

I'm only suggesting you be general if this is your first experience with this type of request. If you believe the universe delivers, ask away!

3. Ask that when your request arrives it is made *obvious* to you. (We are being presented with things constantly from the universe, most of which we take for granted and don't acknowledge come from the universe).
    - Choose something that is not a regular occurrence for you.
    - Choose something that hasn't happened in a while.
4. When it arrives, consciously and graciously accept it.
    - Write in your journal what you did and how you felt.
    - If there is a physical memento you can keep, put it on your vision board or take a photo of the situation and put it on your vision board – you want to remember to continue to practise this simple concept.

Once you see that this concept works, keep requesting. Your part in this is to trust that, by putting the request out there and letting it go, it will be delivered. If your request is not delivered, your part is to catch your thoughts and beliefs

T = Trust

that are preventing it from coming. Anything you think or say against the request will slow it down and even prevent it – that's why it's good to start with small or easy items or experiences that don't matter if they come or not (which contributes to them actually coming). When you know what the beliefs stopping your request from being delivered are, remove them (Chapter 10) and try the exercise again.

You've now got a greater incentive to remove your beliefs. Take note of any thoughts that came up during this exercise and make a note in your BIYB workbook.

Exercise 2

Delegation takes practice

Another way of recognising your ability (or lack thereof) to trust is by delegating a work task that you would normally do yourself. If delegating is something you do on a regular basis you can still test yourself by delegating a task you would *never* usually delegate. If delegating is not on your radar now is the time to put it there.

You don't need to have staff to complete this exercise. That's not a way out. Delegate to a contractor or somebody on Fiverr or Airtasker. If you do have staff, choose somebody you've not delegated to before. Try to remain removed from the person, don't micro-manage or even contact them until the work is done. This creates an even greater aspect to the challenge.

> *Know your lemon juice: While you are going through this process of deciding what you will delegate, which person you will hand the task to, how you feel once the job has been handed over, how often you think about the job, to the point of the job being completed, make a note of all the thoughts, feelings and actions you take. That's the information that will lead to your underlying beliefs connected to trust.*

Exercise 3
One day becomes day one

Select something from your 'one day' list in the Measures chapter and take a step towards it. For example, if you intend to learn a new language, begin by researching all the ways you could learn (online course, at a local college, teach yourself via YouTube) plus any costs or logistics you need to be aware of. This process alone will begin to eliminate any excuses you have to not do it yet. Your thoughts and beliefs will be in over-drive at this point, throwing you reasons why you can't start yet, so catch as many of them as you can. Trust yourself and start.

T = Trust

Post-exercise suggestion: *On completion of the exercises you will have a list of beliefs, thoughts, feelings and actions around this particular topic that you are now consciously aware of. Your objective is to discover the underlying belief(s). If you are not sure what the belief is, you can go back to the section called Exploring Your Own Thoughts in Chapter 3 to explore the thought some more. Once you have a list of beliefs, you can choose to manage, change or remove them. How to do this is outlined in Chapter 10.*

'We are what we repeatedly do. Success is not an action but a habit.'

Aristotle, ancient Greek philosopher and scientist, 384 BC – 322BC.

H
= Habits

Chapter 9
The Winds of Change

Intellectually *knowing* something will *not* create the change – it's the action that creates the change and repeating that action forms a habit.

The power of the mind continues to surprise scientists and researchers all over the world. Neuroplasticity is a relatively new discovery showing that your brain can rewire itself in order to learn something new. Your beliefs are not set in stone – they can and do change depending on your awareness of them. The placebo concept continues to generate outcomes once perceived impossible. It *is* possible to teach an old dog new tricks and the brain will literally rewire itself so that the new trick becomes your new normal.

The greatest challenge you face when wanting to change something is the voice of resistance or your lemon juice. Generally speaking, people don't like change. We like to feel comfortable – hence we each live within our individual comfort zones. However, in order to grow and develop yourself and your business you need to go where you haven't been before and wherever that is, it is outside of your comfort zone

If you decided to run a marathon you would prepare yourself over a period of time, starting with short runs and a possible change in diet. You'd build that up over time with gradual changes until your body became used to running a long distance and you were prepared. The same applies to forming a new habit, which usually means challenging an old habit and starting something new. We've all experienced the New Year's resolution that lasted until 10 January!

A long held habit becomes an addiction that if required to cease can cause trauma by disrupting your norm. Your addiction doesn't have to be to drugs or alcohol to create a traumatic effect on the body. Something as simple as getting up an hour earlier or having a juice for breakfast instead of a coffee will trigger many new responses in your body. Habits are your attachment to doing something that is familiar, safe (in that it keeps you in a place you know) and comfortable. This is something that (you think) you have control of.

H = Habits

This chapter gives you a series of small, reasonably insignificant changes to make to gently disrupt your everyday habits and get you comfortable with being uncomfortable. Once your subconscious mind, the part that *loves* habits, *is* the voice of resistance and works on auto pilot, has grown accustomed to things changing, change will become easier. Any change, regardless of size, is made up of smaller changes and in time the big change will be achieved. No big change happens in one step – some happen quicker than others but rarely in one step.

As a business leader, you are constantly growing, looking for inspiration from others who have gone before you and generally open to being the best you can be. Getting used to the business environment changing is a must; training yourself to adapt and change is your choice.

Today, with access to the Internet, it's possible to find out everything about successful people: how many hours they work, how they tackle challenges, their daily routines, all the things *you* deal with on a daily basis. If you're going to change a habit or create a new one, make it something that will benefit your business, too.

The following exercises are ways to prepare you to step out of your comfort zone to where the magic happens – and it all begins with a toothbrush!

Pre-exercise suggestion: *Prior to beginning any of the exercises, use the BIYB Workbook which you can download from www.believeinyourbusiness.info or, if you don't have the workbook, have a piece of paper or notebook available to answer the questions and catch those first, fleeting thoughts and beliefs. You may perceive them as reasons you don't have to do a specific exercise (aka excuses). If that's how they come to you, still jot them down. You could possibly get a feeling like dread or anxiety or even elation or excitement; or you may find yourself physically avoiding the exercise by leaving the room to get another drink. This, too, is vital information, so write it down. The more you can capture of what is going on in your mind and body when confronted with particular tasks, the more lemon juice you will discover.*

Exercise 1

Clean your teeth with your opposite hand!

Yes, you are going to start with the mundane but essential task of cleaning your teeth. If you usually use your right hand to clean your teeth I'm suggesting you swap hands and start using your left. This also includes using your opposite hand to turn on the tap and to put the toothpaste on your brush.

What you will discover from this simple task is how automatically you usually do this (and many other daily routines). By changing it up a bit you *have* to focus on what you are doing because it is not what your subconscious mind is expecting. This process also forces you to be present, that is, you are only thinking about the task at hand, and

H = Habits

your usual train of thought about the day ahead has been forced to stop while you focus on this new task. What may still get through is the voice of resistance – 'This is too hard', 'This is silly', 'How's this going to help me grow my business?' Keep at it – the purpose is to *get comfortable with being uncomfortable.*

After a week of cleaning your teeth using your opposite hand, you can begin to add a second disruption to your regular routine. Get dressed differently. If you normally put your right sock on first, put your left one on first then do the same with your shoes. It sounds very simple when you read it but it will surprise you how much effort it takes at first. Keep changing other things in your daily routine like using your opposite hand to stir your coffee, operate the TV controls, search on your phone, or operate your mouse. All of these are great to get you out of auto pilot and familiar with consciously making decisions and focusing.

These are the first steps of training for your marathon. The more comfortable you are with being uncomfortable the easier it becomes to make new decisions.

> *Know your lemon juice: Keep a note of how easily (or not) it is for you to operate consciously and how long you can remain focused.*

Exercise 2
Leave your phone at home

I can hear your voice of resistance. Yes, this is a big one for a lot of us, especially if you run your own business. However, you can break this down into smaller chunks to start with, if you prefer. How about turning your phone off for one hour? Then increase that to two hours until you can work up to a full day.

Why? Because the purpose is to disrupt your normal. My phone fell out of my jeans back pocket into the loo recently and once I'd stopped laughing my whole contacts list flashed before me. It took forty-eight hours for me to get re-connected and during that time *I didn't miss out on anything*!

For those of us of a certain age we've lived without carrying our world in our hand so we know that life is possible without a mobile phone. Having said that, using a phone for almost everything is a very easy convenience to become addicted to and dependent on.

During the forty-eight hours I was without a phone I went from an initial panic (not huge) to accepting that yes, it's inconvenient but the people who need to find me can (nobody needed to!). I also realised how often I went to pick my phone up just to look at Facebook (another habit/addiction).

> *Know your lemon juice: The thought of this exercise is enough for some people's minds to fill with justifiable reasons why they can't possibly do this exercise. Do it anyway!*

Exercise 3
Decide to change a habit

Once you have been practising changing some of your automatic behaviours as suggested in Exercise 1, you will have started to gently awaken your conscious mind and should find focusing easier. Because you are unlikely to be emotionally attached or invested in cleaning your teeth or getting dressed differently, you have probably managed to do them quite easily and have laughed at yourself because sometimes something so simple felt so hard.

Now it's time for you to choose something that *you* would like to change. Start with something you will be able to ease into. Don't go too big too soon.

Below is an example of how I suggest you approach changing a habit you *really* want to change.

This example is intentionally not directly business related, as there are too many variables, however, the concept applies to changing any habit.

The habit you wish to change: To stop drinking alcohol.

Step 1: Make three lists.

A list of *why* you want to stop drinking.

A list of the way your life *will be* when you have stopped drinking.

A list of how you will *feel* when you have stopped drinking.

These lists don't have to be long. One reason is enough, but if you have more list them all.

Your reasons *why* could be you want to save the money you usually spend on alcohol. Or you want to lose some weight or get into shape, and this would help. Or you have an illness and you need to stop drinking.

How life *will be* when you have stopped drinking could be that you are able to go on a holiday with the money you have saved. Or you will be able to enjoy wearing certain clothes, or even begin to play sport (again). Or you will be healthy again.

How you *feel* could include being excited about having extra money, or feeling more confident in not having

H = Habits

to hide your body, or feeling well and full of energy again.

Step 2: Set some targets (not in stone)
For example, if you have a drink every night, begin by choosing one night a week that you don't drink at all. Once that becomes comfortable, choose a second night that you don't drink at all. Once that becomes doable, select another day and either stop or reduce the amount you drink that day (from two glasses to just one). Making changes with small steps is a lot easier than going cold turkey. Hopefully you can see that if you gradually ease into it, it is a manageable process. If you don't stick to it every day, don't give up. We all have bad days, start again the next day.

Whatever it is you want to change usually involves two parts – stopping something old and starting something new. The secret is to know *why* you want to do it and then begin doing it gradually. In this example the stopping is the drinking, the starting could be the saving money. If your focus can be on what is being gained or the benefits, not the loss, your subconscious mind won't fight as much. Your RAS is responding to your thoughts, so thinking about what you are starting will produce more positive outcomes than thinking about what you are losing.

If you were to wake up tomorrow morning and declare to yourself, 'I don't drink alcohol anymore,' every cell in your body would begin to crave alcohol, firstly, because you mentioned it and secondly, because we fight things that change drastically. It is definitely possible to change a habit this way but it can be very challenging.

My own habit-changing experiment

A couple of years ago I decided I wanted to see if I could stop drinking coffee and alcohol. I didn't have to and I didn't need to. I literally just wanted to test my willpower – that was my why. At the time, I only drank one coffee a day, which I bought from a café in the morning and my alcohol intake was on average only four glasses of red wine a week over four nights. So the challenge didn't appear too great.

I would purchase my coffee on the way back from walking my dog on the beach. At first I had to force myself to drive straight home and not stop for my coffee. Then one day I started to count the days I'd managed to survive without a coffee and that became my new focus. I did occasionally have one cup and, as much as I enjoyed it, I became more interested in my personal challenge of testing my willpower.

My alcohol intake wasn't huge. On average, I would have a glass of red wine with or after my dinner, four nights a week. It wasn't even the same four nights. The first thing I did was stop buying the bottle of wine when I did my weekly shop. At first this didn't have any effect because I would pick one up on the way home from work. On the evenings when there wasn't any wine I survived and eventually got into the habit of *not* having a glass of wine with or after dinner.

I found the most challenging part was the change in routine over my craving for either drink. My taste buds enjoyed my morning coffee and my evening glass of red and replacing them with a different drink did not work for me. I stopped both at the same time for a period of eighteen months and now I *consciously choose* whether to have a coffee and very rarely have a glass of wine. If I were told I could never have either again it would not be a problem.

In hindsight, this exercise showed me that it definitely wasn't the actual drinks alone that had created the habit, rather it was the experience and the associations connected to them. My visit to the café was enjoyable because I knew the staff and we would have a chat. I'd take my coffee home to my office and would begin work. I would always sip my coffee and make it last. I would hold my coffee cup when I needed some think time. My habit had become greater than the coffee itself. My glass of wine also became more than just the wine. I would enjoy sitting curled up watching a film or I'd do some journaling while I drank my wine. Or sometimes I would use that time to reflect on my day.

So don't be disheartened if you struggle at first because your habit could be associated with a lot more than you realise.

If you have begun to feel comfortable with brushing your teeth with your opposite hand and you've managed to switch your phone off for a couple of hours a day your subconscious mind will be getting comfortable with change. Keep making small changes in your day or week and then apply your newfound comfort with change to something you've been putting off or something you've been too scared to attempt. Now is the best time to step where you have never been before. Another gradual change will not feel so disruptive.

Please note: you may find it easier if you have someone to be accountable to, like a support buddy. Don't be afraid to ask someone to help you. They may also want to join you and change one of their habits, too. If you don't have someone to support you, create your own chart with your *why*, *will be* and *feel* on it to motivate you. Tick off the days you've been successful and allow yourself a few set backs on the way!

Good luck!

> *Know your lemon juice: Keeping notes on how you feel while considering and then actioning Exercise 3 will show you a great deal about yourself and possibly how protective you are about your habits. Write everything down and find those beliefs.*

The Winds of Change

Post-exercise suggestion: *On completion of the exercises you will have a list of beliefs, thoughts, feelings and actions around this particular topic that you are now consciously aware of. Your objective is to discover the underlying belief(s). If you are not sure what the belief is, you can go back to the section called Exploring Your Own Thoughts in Chapter 3 to explore the thought some more. Once you have a list of beliefs, you can choose to manage, change or remove them. How to do this is outlined in Chapter 10.*

'We can change our lives as fast as we can change our beliefs, and since our beliefs can change instantly we can actually change our lives instantly.'

Dr Bruce Lipton, American biologist, 1944.

Chapter 10

Letting Go of Beliefs

This is where the magic happens …

Prior to beginning this process I want to outline my perspective on why I suggest you remove your beliefs.

A belief is a thought you keep thinking until it becomes real or true to you. By the time this has happened, the belief also has emotion attached to it – this applies whether the belief is good or not. Those accumulated emotions act as an indicator for you. If you believe you are scared of spiders and you see a spider you will feel the emotion (fear in this case) that is attached to that belief. Just as if you believe you love kittens and you see a litter of kittens you will feel the emotion (love in this case) that is attached to that belief.

That belief (enveloped in emotion) is taking up space in your body, similar to the analogy I used earlier of a boulder in a flowing river. The boulder doesn't stop the river from flowing but it does cause it to flow in a certain direction. If the boulder were to be removed the river would flow more freely. Your energy also flows in a certain direction to accommodate the beliefs you have.

If you *remove* a belief and associated emotion you create space for your energy to flow more freely. If you *replace* a belief with a new one you immediately refill that space. If this space remains clear not only does it allow more energy to flow through you, it keeps you relatively neutral on particular subjects and enables you to be open to new perspectives.

This concept insinuates that all beliefs are restricting in some way as they limit your thinking and create conditions. A very simple example could be a person believes, *I never win anything*, and so chooses to replace that belief with a more positive one, for example, *I always win.* This *appears* to be a good replacement. However, that belief could create self-induced pressure, disappointment or doubt as soon as they *don't* win something.

An ideal state is to not have any beliefs around winning and be able to *accept* the outcome for what it is. Therefore, winning or losing wouldn't be conditional to them. Plus with the space created from the removal of those beliefs the person's intuition/gut feeling would be more prominent.

Once you have experienced both removing and replacing your own beliefs you can draw your own conclusion as to what you feel is best for you.

Preparation

Have your list of all the beliefs you've discovered from each of the G.R.O.W.T.H exercises where you can reach it. If there are beliefs you would like to replace, list the replacement belief next to the current belief.

The beliefs you choose to remove or change can be positive or negative. Remember: your beliefs are keeping you safe, so even the positive sounding ones could be causing a restriction. If you release a belief and then wish you hadn't, you just think it again.

What you will discover through this process of removing a belief is how much room the belief takes up in your body. When you see this for yourself you will realise that the belief (positive or negative) is restricting the flow of energy through your body. Be aware that if you choose to replace a belief you are refilling that space again – even though it's with a better belief.

The more beliefs you remove from your body the less you will have to worry about because you won't be hoping something happens in a certain way, you will just accept that it happens. This is also known as going with the flow and being present. I am sure you have experienced going with the flow at some stage of your life. If you haven't, it's that time when everything just seems to be unfolding perfectly and effortlessly: the right person turns up, you receive some money just in time to pay the bill, you catch that perfect wave you've been chasing forever – these type of scenarios are good indicators that you are in flow. That flow is partly due to you being free of control/rules/conditions and being in a mindset of accepting whatever happens. With some effort, you can be in flow much more often.

Process

I have developed three different processes to remove a belief, each one slightly different from the others. Try all three and choose the one that resonates with you the most.

Process 1: **Breathe**

1. Find a comfortable, quiet place to sit.
2. Remove any potential distractions – phone, pets, or people.
3. Have your list of beliefs on your lap or next to you.
4. Choose one belief from your list – positive or negative.
5. Close your eyes and slowly say the belief to yourself at least five times.
6. Think the belief.

Letting Go of Beliefs

7. Imagine a time when that belief caused you to feel those emotions (good or bad), picture yourself back there and let yourself experience the situation again.
8. Allow your body to *feel* the emotion around the belief.
9. Now, scan your body. (Scanning your body means while keeping your eyes closed, you *look* at your body from head to toe.) Can you find where that belief is sitting in your body? This may sound strange but every belief is inside your body somewhere. Listen to your body and it will show you where the belief is. What you are feeling is the emotion surrounding the belief. If this takes a bit of time, persevere – it is worth it.
10. If you cannot find the belief in your body, continue to say the belief to yourself, think it and feel it.
11. If you still cannot find that belief, gently open your eyes and select another from your list and go through the process to this point again.
12. When you have found it, explore it. See if you can observe the following:

    - How big is it?
    - What shape is it?
    - What colour is it?
    - Does it have a texture?
    - Can you see all its edges?
    - Can you see anything else about it?
    - (Take your time doing the above as this allows you to really focus on it.)

13. Now, using your imagination, bring that shape (belief) to your throat. Imagine it moving through your body to your throat. Be patient, it will happen.

14. Take a long breath in through your nose, filling your belly.
15. Then open your mouth and breathe the shape (belief) out slowly.
16. You may even want to cough it out and that's OK.
17. You may feel like making a sound as you breathe out.
18. As you breathe it out, the belief dissipates into the air.
19. If the whole shape (belief) does not leave your body in one breath, take another long breath in through your nose and out through your mouth, releasing more of the belief.
20. You can repeat this process until that particular belief has been removed.

Sometimes not all of the shape (belief) will leave your body in the first attempt. You can go through the process steps again and release the remainder of the shape now, or you can go back and release it at another time.

1. Now take your attention to the space where the belief was before you removed it.
2. Imagine a white light coming in through the top of your head, down through your body and into that space, filling it. This light will merge with your energy.
3. If you are choosing to replace the belief with a new one, focus on the space, say the new belief and see the new belief filling the space.

If you felt this process worked easily for you, you can move on to the next belief on your list that you wish to remove.

Depending on how you feel, you can keep going through your list. If you feel you need to stop, then do. Some of the beliefs you remove may have been with you for ten or twenty years, so even though the exercise appears simple, it could have a strong impact on your body. I have experienced clients feeling nauseous and drained after removing just one belief, so be aware of how you are feeling. If you feel funny, stop, get some air, a glass of water and sit quietly. Only continue if you feel you can.

I suggest you revisit this exercise again approximately four to six hours after you first do it. Use the same list of beliefs and check they are no longer in your body. If they have all gone, great work, you did it. If some have reappeared or you only managed to remove some of the shape (belief) the first time around, go back to the beginning of the process and re-do it. If you find the same belief is still there, don't dismiss what you are doing as not working. As I mentioned above, some of these beliefs have been with you for a long time and have shaped your life, so removing them may take a few attempts.

The Breathe process is my favourite as it can be carried out quite discretely once you are used to the process. If you find yourself realising a belief before you are about to go into a meeting or give a talk on stage, you can take yourself through this process and either cough or breathe out without drawing attention to yourself. It's a great process to turn into a habit.

Process 2: **Juggling**

For this technique you need something to throw. I suggest a juggling ball or a hacky sack because they are a good size and are soft, squishy and don't bounce. If you don't have a juggling ball or hacky sack use something similar like a rolled up pair of socks or a ball of wool. If you have two or three of them that would be good but one is sufficient.

1. Sit on a chair about one metre from a blank wall, facing the wall. Make sure there are no windows or doors close by. (You can sit anywhere but you are going to throw the juggling ball and you don't want it to break anything or rebound and hit you.)
2. Hold the juggling ball (or alternative soft item) in your dominant hand (put any additional ones in your lap).
3. Remove any potential distractions – phone, pets, or people.
4. Have your list of beliefs on your lap or next to you.
5. Choose one belief from your list – positive or negative.
6. Close your eyes and slowly say the belief to yourself at least five times.
7. Think the belief.
8. Imagine a time when that belief caused you to feel those emotions (good or bad), picture yourself back there and let yourself experience the situation again.

Letting Go of Beliefs

9. Allow your body to *feel* the emotion around the belief.
10. Now, scan your body. (Scanning your body means while keeping your eyes closed, you *look* at your body from head to toe.) Can you find where that belief is sitting in your body? This may sound strange but every belief is inside your body somewhere! Listen to your body and it will show you where the belief is. What you are feeling is the emotion surrounding the belief. If this takes a bit of time, persevere – it is worth it.
11. If you cannot find the belief in your body, continue to say the belief to yourself, think it and feel it.
12. If you still cannot find that belief, gently open your eyes and select another from your list and go through the process to this point again.
13. When you have found it, explore it. See if you can observe the following:

    - How big is it?
    - What shape is it?
    - What colour is it?
    - Does it have a texture?
    - Can you see all its edges?
    - Can you see anything else about it?

14. Using your imagination, move the shape (belief) to the shoulder of your dominant hand.
15. Imaging the shape (belief) coming down your arm into the palm of your hand.
16. Squeeze the ball (or alternative soft item) and imagine transferring the shape (belief) into it.
17. Feel the belief being absorbed into the ball (or alternative soft item).
18. Hold the juggling ball tight, keep your eyes closed, and throw the ball down to the floor in front of you

with as much strength as you can. Do not throw it at the wall as it may rebound and hit you.
19. If the whole shape (belief) does not leave your body in one throw, pick up another ball from your lap, bring the shape (belief) into the palm of your hand, feel the belief being absorbed into the ball, squeeze the ball and throw it down to the floor.
20. You can repeat this process until that particular belief has been removed.

Sometimes not all of the shape (belief) will leave your body in the first attempt. You can go through the process steps again and release the remainder of the shape now, or you can go back and release it at another time.

1. Now take your attention to the space where the belief was before you removed it.
2. Imagine a white light coming in through the top of your head, down through your body and into that space, filling it. This light will merge with your energy.
3. If you are choosing to replace the belief with a new one, focus on the space, say the new belief and see the new belief filling the space.

If you felt this process worked easily for you, you can move on to the next belief on your list. Depending on how you feel, you can keep going through your list. If you feel you need to stop then do. Some of the beliefs you remove may have been with you for ten or twenty years, so even though the exercise appears simple, it could have a strong impact on your body.

I have experienced clients feeling nauseous and drained after removing just one belief, so be aware of how you are feeling. If you feel funny, stop, get some air, a glass of water and sit quietly. Only continue if you feel you can.

I suggest you revisit this exercise again approximately four to six hours after you first do it. Use the same list of beliefs and check they are no longer in your body. If they have all gone, great work, you did it. If some have reappeared or you only managed to remove some of the shape (belief) the first time around, go back to the beginning of the process and re-do it. If you find the same belief is still there, don't dismiss what you are doing as not working. As I mentioned above, some of these beliefs have been with you for a long time and have shaped your life, so removing them may take a few attempts.

Process 3: **Sifting**

This process is ideal for those who would prefer to remove their beliefs while lying down. You can lie down on your bed or the floor – wherever you are comfortable. If it's not possible to lie down you can adapt the exercise to a seated position if you prefer this method.

1. Lie comfortably on the bed/floor.
2. Remove any potential distractions – phone, pets, or people.
3. Have your list of beliefs next to you.

4. Imagine you are laying on a piece of gauze the size of a large beach towel. The holes in the gauze are small – similar to a sieve.
5. Choose one belief from your list – positive or negative.
6. Close your eyes and say the belief slowly to yourself a couple of times.
7. Think the belief.
8. Imagine a time when that belief caused you to feel those emotions (good or bad), picture yourself back there and let yourself experience the situation again.
9. Allow your body to *feel* the emotion around the belief.
10. Now scan your body. (Scanning your body means while keeping your eyes closed, you *look* at your body from head to toe.) Can you find where that belief is sitting in your body? This may sound strange but every belief is inside your body somewhere. Listen to your body and it will show you where the belief is. What you are feeling is the emotion surrounding the belief. If this takes a bit of time, persevere – it is worth it.
11. If you cannot find the belief in your body, continue to say the belief to yourself, think it and feel it.
12. If you still cannot find that belief, gently open your eyes and select another from your list and go through the process to this point again.
13. When you have found it, explore it. See if you can observe the following:

- How big is it?
- What shape is it?
- What colour is it?
- Does it have a texture?

- Can you see all its edges?
- Can you see anything else about it?

14. When you feel ready, imagine the gauze you are lying on being lifted in each corner and rising through your body.
15. The gauze acts like a sieve, sifting through your body and collecting in it the belief you are releasing.
16. The gauze is pulled through your whole body.
17. The gauze continues to rise up above you, until you can no longer see it.
18. If the whole shape (belief) does not leave your body in one attempt you can repeat this process until that particular belief has been removed.

Sometimes not all of the shape (belief) will leave your body in the first attempt. You can go through the process steps again and release the remainder of the shape now, or you can go back and release it at another time.

1. Now take your attention to the space where the belief was before you removed it.
2. Imagine a white light coming in through the top of your head, down through your body and into that space, filling it. The light will merge with your energy.
3. If you are choosing to replace the belief with a new one, focus on the space, say the new belief and see the new belief filling the space.

Depending on how you feel, you can keep going through your list. If you feel you need to stop then do. Some of the beliefs you remove may have been with you for ten or twenty years, so even though the exercise appears simple, it could have a strong impact on your body. I have experienced clients feeling nauseous and drained after removing just one belief, so be aware of how you are feeling. If you feel funny, stop, get some air, a glass of water and sit quietly. Only continue if you feel you can.

I suggest you revisit this exercise again approximately four to six hours after you first do it. Use the same list of beliefs and check they are no longer in your body. If they have all gone, great work, you did it. If some have reappeared or you only managed to remove some of the shape (belief) the first time around, go back to the beginning of the process and re-do it. If you find the same belief is still there, don't dismiss what you are doing as not working. As I mentioned above, some of these beliefs have been with you for a long time and have shaped your life, so removing them may take a few attempts.

You can use these techniques over and over again. You will find that you prefer one process more than the others. All of them will successfully remove a belief. If you have a belief that is long-standing and deeply embedded you may have to revisit it a couple of times. Do not give up – removing a belief will make a difference to your life. As stated earlier, if you remove a belief and then wish you hadn't, just start thinking it again. That's all a belief is – a thought you just keep thinking.

How will you know if the belief has successfully been removed or replaced?

The best way for you to discover whether a belief has been removed is to put yourself in a position that will test you. This isn't always possible so you may have to wait to see whether your behaviour is different.

I have found that when a client or I, myself, have removed a belief within a short time – usually no longer than a week – a situation will arise that will *test* that particular belief. When you start doing this regularly, you will often smile at how the universe is constantly guiding us to grow.

I've had clients remove a simple belief around money and within days they have called me to let me know they have raised their prices and can't understand why they hadn't done it sooner. I've had a client say they want to hire a nanny for three days a week but can't afford it. They removed the belief (that they couldn't afford it) and at our next session just one week later, she told me she had found the perfect nanny and the payment was being made in food and lodgings, so no money was even needed. I have many stories showing that the process of removing a belief definitely enables you to move forward.

Another way to check is to scan your body over the next few days (after doing the exercise) and see if the belief is still there. If it is, it is possibly because it is a long-standing, embedded belief and you automatically or subconsciously continued to think it after you had removed it the first time, so it has reappeared. Use one of the processes and remove it again. This does happen, especially with beliefs that have been dominant in your lifestyle. Remember: beliefs are often linked to habits, so if you are continuing the habit the belief can easily return.

'Comfort is the enemy of progress.'

P.T Barnum, showman and founder of the Barnum
and Bailey Circus, 1810-1891.

Chapter 11

Revisiting Your Measures

It's time to revisit the measures you prepared at the beginning of the book, the purpose being to see whether your perspective has shifted. You can choose to complete the exercises again, without referring to your original version, or revisit your original version and make any changes you feel necessary.

Measure 1

The first measure was to write your eulogy. Refer back to your written eulogy. When you read that back to yourself now, having identified and removed some of your old beliefs, how does it sound? How does it make you feel? Does it still ring true? If you're not happy with how it reads now, re-write it or tweak it so that it resonates with you again.

When you are happy with it, you may want to print it out and keep it to refer to again in a few months time once you've begun to see changes in your behaviour, as a result of removing some beliefs and implementing some of the suggested exercises.

Measure 2

Your business comfort zone was the second measure – scoring areas of your business dependent on how you felt each was performing. Although you may not have had time to focus on or implement any ideas towards changing them, you will benefit from revisiting the original scores you allocated to each area. Remember you look at things differently when you feel different. Make any changes you consider necessary and re-read the statements outlining *ideally* how you would like those areas to be. It's good practice to have an *ideal* statement for all areas outlined in your business comfort zone.

Measure 3

This is the 'I love you' exercise. The response I regularly see from this exercise is people either love it or hate it – there's no in-between. So did you love it or hate it? I suggest you do it again even if you felt comfortable the first time around and see if it feels different this time. Do you feel more confident saying it this time? Do you actually believe it when you say it? If first time around you only managed to say I like you not I love you, try it again. If you couldn't even look at yourself in your first attempt, you can build up to this by looking at your face in a mirror. Don't criticise what you see; accept what you see. When you feel comfortable enough look into your eyes. After a while this will feel more comfortable and you can say something to yourself whilst looking into your eyes. Begin with, 'Good morning, how are you today?' and work from there, as though you were talking to a friend. Eventually you will be able to say I love you.

It's important that you don't beat yourself up (metaphorically) over this exercise. For many people it's a very alien thing to do, as it is not something we are taught or observe, which is why it feels strange. The benefits are worth it – you will begin to feel more comfortable being you, your self-worth will grow and you will be nicer to yourself.

Measure 4

This measure was for you to list some of the activities you'd like to do one day. Now that you have completed the G.R.O.W.T.H exercises do you feel differently either about the activities themselves or about the timeframe you gave them? Can you see some of them happening much sooner than you had originally anticipated?

Select one activity or event from your list and start the ball rolling today!

'If you hear a voice within you say, "You cannot paint," then by all means paint and that voice will be silenced.'

Vincent van Gogh, Dutch post-impressionist painter, 1853 – 1890.

Chapter 12

Moving Forward

Because you've completed the G.R.O.W.T.H exercises and to help remind you how far you've come we've created a simple way for you to record your personal highlights from each chapter. This can be used to motivate and inspire you to continue to recognise your beliefs, remove them and continue your journey of growth.

My board of direction

This diagram also printed in the BIYB workbook can be enlarged to any size to create a summary of the significant components from each of the G.R.O.W.T.H areas that resonated with you. It can become a screensaver or poster in your office to keep you focused.

Highlight one or two impacting pieces from the Grounding, Rejection, Outcome, Wealth, Trust and Habit chapters and place them around your boardroom table for motivation.

There's a lot of information to be digested and some areas will process more quickly than others. This diagram is an opportunity for you to interpret your intentions going forward.

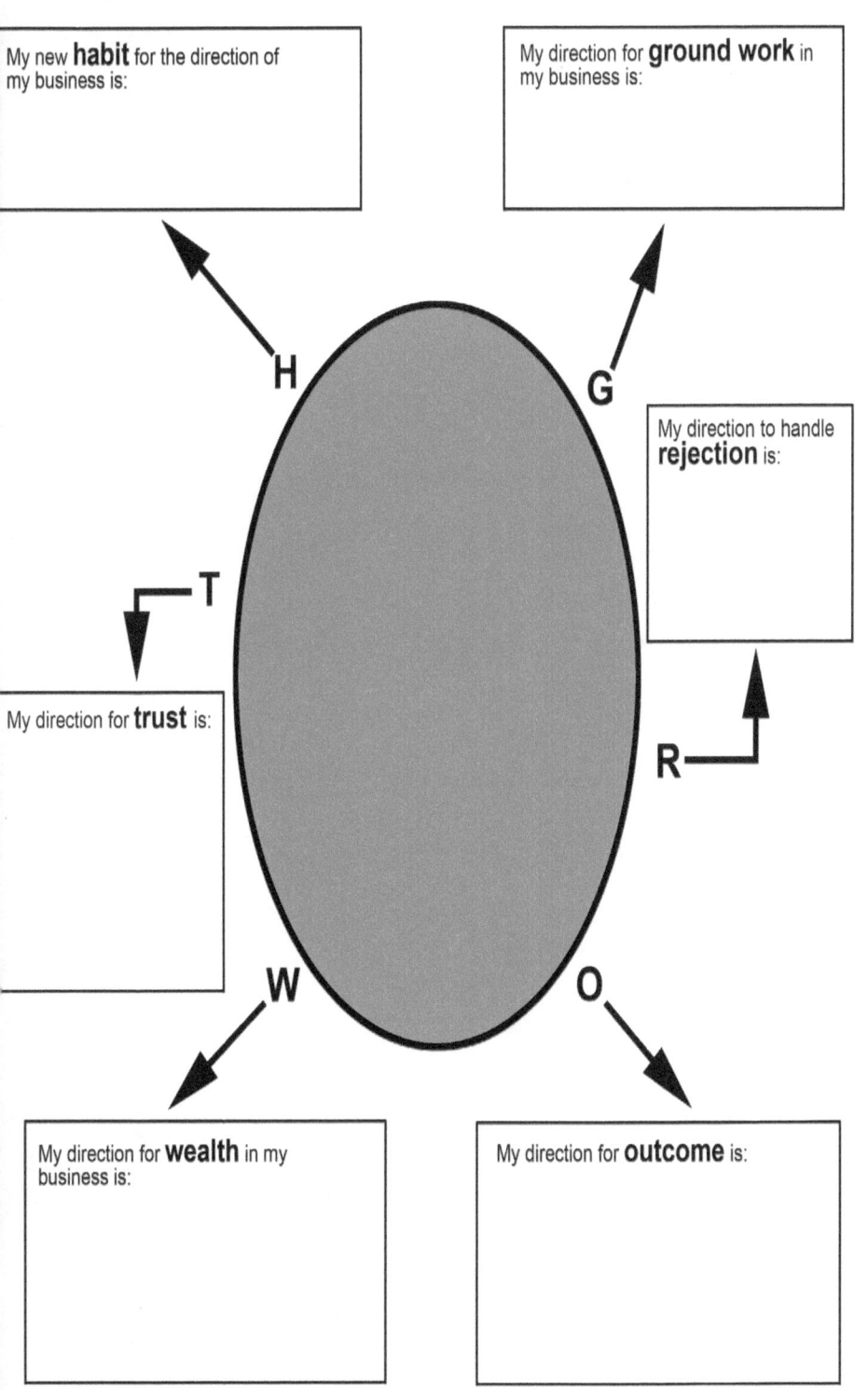

'Every child is an artist. The problem is how to remain an artist once he grows up.'

Pablo Picasso, Spanish artist, 1881 – 1973.

Afterword

Life as a teenager is challenging enough without the added question of, 'What do you want to be when you grow up?' thrown in the mix.

When I was in high school I felt very alone when it came to decisions about my future. I felt I lacked guidance and was unsure of what options I had. I didn't have the clarity some of my friends had – they knew exactly what they wanted to be. Throughout our school years, my best friend, Mandy, wanted to be a vet or a policewoman – she became a policewoman. I couldn't decide between a window dresser or fashion designer, however my art teacher decided that for me when, at just thirteen years old, she told me in front of my classmates that I couldn't draw and that I couldn't select art as an elective subject. As a young person, the significance that authority figure had on my creative confidence remained hidden for a long time. I didn't question her – she was the art teacher, she knew. As for being given this devastating news in front of my classmates, the humiliation ensured I wouldn't be being creative any time soon.

Once I'd left school it didn't stop me from making all the soft furnishings in my homes and clothes for lots of my friends in the 80s – the era of huge shoulder pads – but it did stop me from pursuing a creative career. I was led to believe that not having a piece of paper (certificate) meant the end of any possible fashion or creative career. I had been too afraid to question authority and so I put that dream to bed. It wouldn't be until twenty-five years later, during my first trip to Australia, that my confidence in my creativity was restored. I attended a casual screen-printing class in Perth and the art teacher asked me where I had learnt to draw!

In hindsight, I thought somebody else was going to tell me or show me or guide me towards the choices I had. When I realised that wasn't forthcoming and that I was on my own I leaned back towards what my parents perceived as a good job and became a bank teller.

This time in my life left me with a desire to help other teens through this period of change. I'm happy to say that this book is the start of formalising that desire with AUD$2.00 from the sale of each book being donated to Freelance Australia (FA). More information about FA can be found on the following pages.

Those feelings have never quite left me and are one of the reasons I love mentoring. Having just one person believe in you is enough to give you the confidence to keep going. It's an honour and privilege to work with business owners, encouraging them to trust their instincts and follow those feelings, being a sounding board and helping them connect with people who can further help them. We're not alone; we just have to ask.

As for the *creative career* I buried all those years ago, the more beliefs I remove the closer to the surface it rises. Through mentoring I have seen that turning a passion into a business can sometimes dilute the passion so now I enjoy upholstering old furniture without the pressure of it being a business and in fact it is my meditation.

'You must expect great things of yourself before you can do them.'

Michael Jordan, American basketball player, born 1963.

Freelance Australia Pty Ltd

From the sale of every copy of *Believe in your Business* AUD$2.00 will be donated to Freelance Australia Pty Ltd.

Freelance Australia is a not-for-profit organisation whose mission is to represent the collective interests of Australian freelancers, contractors and independent workers. Its goal is to encourage the development and proliferation of better, happier and more successful freelancers as society progresses towards a new future of work. This future of work depends on the next generation of thinkers, doers and – most importantly – believers to shape it in new and meaningful ways.

Your support of this book will help the next generation tune into their unique and inherent voice through programs that will teach them to become professionally independent. A belief program tailored to 13 – 17 year olds will be developed specifically with the donated funds.

Thank you for your contribution.

More information can be found here:

facebook.com/freelanceau

twitter.com/freelanceorgau

instagram.com/freelanceau

'Beauty begins the moment you decide to be yourself.'

Coco Chanel, fashion designer and businesswoman, 1883-1971.

References

American Express 2017, *The 2017 States of Women-owned Businesses Report*, American Express

BetterHealth Channel, *Body Image – Men*, Victorian Government

Braden, Gregg 2008, *The Spontaneous Healing of Belief*, Hay House

Chander, Raj 2018, 'With Superheroes Comes the Pressure of Unrealistic Male Bodies', *HealthLine*, <healthline.com>

Cuddy, Amy 2015, *Presence*, Hachette UK, United Kingdom

Dispenza, Joe 2014, *You Are the Placebo: Making your mind matter*, Hay House

Dove 2017, *Girls and Beauty Confidence: The Global Report*, Unilever, <unilever.com>

Emmons, Robert & McCullough, Michael 2003, *Highlights from the Research Project on Gratitude and Thankfulness*, University of California & University of Miami, <http://local.psy.miami.edu>

Lipton, Bruce H 2016, *The Biology of Belief: Unleash the power of your mind to take control of your life and your health*, Hay House

Morrissey, Mary 2016, 'The Power of Writing Down Your Goals and Dreams', *HuffPost*, <huffpost.com>

The National Institute for Play, <nifplay.org>

Steven 2018, 'Message from the Dean – December 10, 2018', *Broncho Blogs*, <blogs.uco.edu>

Tattersall, Hannah 2018, 'Women of Influence 2018: Surge in entries from entrepreneurs and small business', *Financial Review*, <afr.com>

TheOffice 2015, 'Brene Brown on Creativity', *TheOffice*, <theofficeonline.com>

Zetlin, Minda 2018, 'Money Can Really Buy Happiness If You Spend It These Four Ways, According to Science', *Inc*, <inc.com>

References

Additional Reading/Listening

Some additional reading and TED Talks you may find interesting:

Books

The Biology of Beliefs	Bruce H Lipton
Chapter One: You Have the Power to Change Stuff	Daniel Flynn
The Happiness Advantage	Shawn Achor
Loneliness: Human Nature and the Need for Social Connection	John Cacioppo
Luxury Fever: Why Money Fails to Satisfy in an Era of Excess	Robert H Frank
The Magic of Believing (1948)	Claude M Bristol
My Stroke of Insight: A Brain Scientist's Personal Journey	Jill Bolte Taylor
Play: How it Shapes the Brain, Opens the Imagination and Invigorates the Soul	Stuart Brown
The Power of Vulnerability	Brene Brown
Presence	Amy Cuddy
Think and Grown Rich	Napoleon Hill
The Untrue Story of You	Bryan Hubbard
The Virgin Way: How to Listen, Learn, Laugh and Lead	Richard Branson
Why Good Things Happen to Good People	Stephen Post & Jill Neimark
You Are the Placebo	Dr Joe Dispenza
You'll See it When You Believe it	Dr Wayne W Dyer

TED Talks

The Happy Secret to Better Work, 2012	Shawn Achor
How Great Leaders Inspire Action, 2012	Simon Sinek
Play, 2009	Stuart Brown
The Power of Vulnerability, 2010	Brene Brown
Your Body Language May Shape Who You Are, 2012	Amy Cuddy

The professional services used

Andrew MacIndoe of MacIndoe Media

www.macindoemedia.com

www.facebook.com/Macindoemedia/

www.linkedin.com/in/andrew-macindoe/

www.instagram.com/macindoemedia/

andy@macindoemedia.com

KBK Digital Marketing

www.linkedin.com/in/katherine-karvess-4a09a02b/

'No one else is you and that is your power.'

Dave Grohl, singer, songwriter, musician and director, born 1969.

About the author

Gaynor Lawton is a belief strategist. Born in the UK, she now lives permanently in Melbourne, Australia with her daughter, dog and cat.

She mentors clients around the world through both personal and business situations with a specific focus on their belief system.

This work has developed as a result of her own life experiences and a lot of observation and awareness of what makes some people appear *lucky* and some *unlucky* when it comes to business success. She has always had a fascination as to what makes people tick.

As a keen reader of autobiographies, she discovered a long time ago that no one is immune to fear and self-doubt – it comes down to some people learning to manage it and others succumbing to its power and living in a restricted environment.

Gaynor's background includes over thirty years working in marketing, event management and corporate fundraising in the UK and Australia, plus running her own marketing and mentoring business for over fourteen years.

In her spare time you'll find her in her shed upholstering old furniture or walking her dog on the many beaches on the beautiful Mornington Peninsula in Victoria, Australia.

www.ingramcontent.com/pod-product-compliance
Lightning Source LLC
Chambersburg PA
CBHW031107080526
44587CB00011B/860